secrets of the blessed man

PAUL TASSELL

REGULAR BAPTIST PRESS
1300 North Meacham Road
Post Office Box 95500
Schaumburg, Illinois 60195

Library of Congress Cataloging in Publication Data

Tassell, Paul, 1934-
  Secrets of the blessed man.
    1. Christian life—Baptist authors.   I. Title.
BV4501.2.T265   248'.48'61   78-22065
ISBN 0-87227-033-5

SECRETS OF THE BLESSED MAN
© 1966
Regular Baptist Press
Schaumburg, Illinois
Printed in the U.S.A.

Second printing—1971
Third printing—1979

Psa. 34:6

Paul Tassell (signature)

secrets
of the
Blessed
man

Mary E. Anderson (signature)

Contents

Preface

"MAY GOD bless you!" How many times have you heard that statement? It is a benediction given by radio announcers, television entertainers, politicians and even preachers. "May God bless you!" But what do people mean when they say this? Perhaps they are hoping to attract God's good favor by invoking His blessing on someone else. Maybe they are trying to impress others with their piety. Or it may be that they are sincerely honest when they say, "God bless you!"

Years ago I heard the late Christian lawyer from New York City, Dr. James Bennett, say: "Never say, 'God bless you' to anyone. You really have no right to do this. What you should say is, 'May you always be found in the place where God can bless you.'"

Dr. Bennett was right. But how can you be sure you are in the place where God can bless you? I believe Psalm 1 adequately answers that most important question. "Blessed is the man that . . ." and then follows the psalmist's formula for being in the place where God can bless you.

Having pastored a church in a university community and after serving as National Youth Representative for the General Association of Regular Baptist Churches and now having the opportunity to speak on a number of college campuses each year, I have found that "success" is the goal of most young people. But to the Christian student, success is more than the ability to hold down a good position or demand a high salary. Success to the Christian is doing the will of God and thereby receiving the blessing of God. The scores of students whom I have the privilege of counseling are interested in practical, workable answers to life's questions and challenges. I have found that the formula for spiritual success given by the writer of Psalm 1 is as workable a road map for life as can be found anywhere.

"The Blessed Man" is a practical man, a man whose life is devoted to the will and work of the Lord. In the pages of this book I have endeavored to present a practical exposition of Psalm 1. I wholeheartedly believe that the Word of God is "a lamp unto my feet, and a light unto my path." If anyone is to live a life that is truly blessed of God, that life must be governed and guided by "Thus saith the Lord." Now—may God bless you as you read about "The Blessed Man!"

Paul Tassell

Grandview Park Baptist Church
Des Moines, Iowa
1978

BLESSED SEPARATION

I. Blessed Because of His Counsel

    A. Counselors should be men of scriptural principles.

    B. Counselors should be men of sensible practicality.

    C. Counselors should be men of sound purpose.

II. Blessed Because of His Conviction

    A. Example of John Hus—through death

    B. Example of Martin Luther—through denial

    C. Example of Daniel—through dens

    D. Example of Moses—through drudgery

III. Blessed Because of His Companionship

    A. The scorners defined.

    B. The scorners described.

    C. The scorners denounced.

CHAPTER ONE

Blessed Separation

"Blessed is the man that walketh not in the counsel of the ungodly, nor standeth in the way of sinners, nor sitteth in the seat of the scornful" (Ps.1:1).

BEFORE WE examine the psalmist's formula for a blessed life, we must first realize that no one can truly be a recipient of this blessedness until he has first become a recipient of the gift of God, which is eternal life through Jesus Christ our Lord. In other words, the life of blessedness is an exclusive life. It is only for God's children. To become a child of God it is necessary to be born into His family. The Lord Jesus Christ said, "Except a man be born again, he cannot see the kingdom of God" (John 3:3). We must be born again because by nature we are "children of disobedience" and "children of wrath," writes the apostle Paul in Ephesians 2:2 and 3. Thus, it is necessary to be "born from above." This takes place for the individual when he accepts the Lord Jesus Christ as his own personal Lord and Savior. John explains it for us: "But as many as received him [Christ], to them gave he power to become the sons of God, even to them that believe on his name" (John 1:12).

Now, having received the Lord Jesus Christ, one is a child of God and a candidate for the life of blessedness which the psalmist has outlined for us in Psalm 1. The Blessed Man can say with the apostle Paul concerning God: "Who hath delivered us from the power of darkness, and hath translated us into the kingdom of his dear Son" (Col. 1:13). So it is that the Blessed Man knows the truth of Biblical separation. He has been delivered or separated *from* one kingdom and translated or separated *unto* another kingdom, even the kingdom of God's dear Son.

Separation is not a very popular word today, but it is a blessed word in the Bible. Paul writes that he was "separated unto the gospel of God" (Rom. 1:1). Christian separation is part of what James calls "pure religion." "Pure religion and undefiled before God and the Father is this, To visit the fatherless and widows in their affliction, and to keep himself unspotted from the world" (James 1:27). James affirms that service and separation complement each other. It is possible to help the sinner without participating in his sin.

The Blessed Man is one who is *in* the world but not *of* the world. The psalmist describes him as one who keeps himself unspotted from the world. He refuses to walk in the counsel of the ungodly. He does not stand in the way of sinners. He will not sit in the seat of the scornful. He believes in living a holy life in the midst of an unholy world. He follows in the train of Enoch, who walked with God rather than follow the counsel of the ungodly. He follows the example of Noah, who separated himself unto an ark and thereby saved himself and his family from destruction. He follows Elijah, who was separated unto the Brook Cherith for fellowship with God instead of mingling in the company of the prophets of Baal and wicked Ahab.

Blessed separation is both negative and positive. We are separated *from* something *to* Someone! But let us not be afraid of the negative side. Have you noticed that the psalmist begins this First Psalm in a negative manner? Blessed is the man that "walketh *not* . . . *nor* standeth . . . *nor* sitteth." Nothing is really wrong with so-called "negative preaching." It is not wrong to warn your child of that which will injure or harm him. Preaching that does not have a negative emphasis is not *practical* preaching. Preaching that does not stress the sinfulness of sin is not *realistic* preaching. And preaching that does not warn and rebuke is not *honest* preaching. And, believe me, tomorrow's leaders, our college young people, want preaching that is practical, realistic and honest if they want any preaching at all. We who are preachers will fail our generation if we do not tell them the truth, the *whole* truth and nothing but the truth!

Biblically true, positive preaching must include Biblically true, negative preaching. Jeremiah was told to "root out, and to pull down, and to destroy, and to throw down." He was also commanded to "build, and to plant" (Jer. 1:10). A proper balance is desperately needed in our ministry of the Word today. The world is unbalanced in its thinking and reeling from the intoxication of its own self-righteousness. The Holy Spirit is here not only to convict of righteousness, but also of sin and judgment. May we never forget this.

Having said this, let us examine the psalmist's viewpoint of blessed separation.

I. Blessed Because of His Counsel

"Blessed is the man that walketh not in the counsel of the ungodly." The Blessed Man has sound advisors. The wise writer of Proverbs says: "Where no counsel is, the people fall: but in the multitude of counsellors there is safety" (Prov. 11:14). How good to have wise counsel! But how tragic to be falsely led by unsound counsel.

Where you go for advice is of great consequence. The people of the United States of America always watch with great interest the choosing of a new president's cabinet. Who will be the secretary of state? What kind of man is he? Is his judgment sound? Has he had successful experience in dealing with problems of an international scope? What about the secretary of the treasury? And others. The people watch these choices of the new president closely because the president's cabinet members will be his advisors and counselors. To a great degree, the president's own wisdom is reflected in the choices he makes for advisors. And your choice of counselors is also a reflection of your own wisdom. Therefore, the psalmist says, "Blessed is the man that walketh not in the counsel of the ungodly."

The United States is a land of newspapers. And almost all of these newspapers have advice columns of one kind or another. It is sad that millions of Americans can find no better place to find help than a newspaper psychologist. Thousands of Americans spend more thousands of dollars every year on horoscope books and magazines. If this is not bad enough, think of the many many people who visit so-called fortune tellers in order to find relief from their burdened minds and hearts. Their counsel is woefully inadequate.

A Christian man has a responsibility before God to be careful in his selection of counselors. He ought to be choosy in his advice-seeking. He should not walk in fellowship with those whose hearts and minds have not been transformed by the grace of God. The apostle Paul writes this pertinent command to the Corinthian believers:

> Be ye not unequally yoked together with unbelievers: for what fellowship hath righteousness with unrighteousness? and what communion hath light with darkness?
> And what concord hath Christ with Belial? or what part hath he that believeth with an infidel?
> And what agreement hath the temple of God with idols? for ye are the temple of the living God; as God hath said, I will dwell in them, and walk in them; and I will be their God, and they shall be my people.
> Wherefore come out from among them, and be ye separate, saith the Lord, and touch not the unclean thing; and I will receive you,
> And will be a Father unto you, and ye shall be my sons and daughters, saith the Lord Almighty (2 Cor. 6:14-18).

Paul is saying, "What good is it for a Christian to go to the Devil for advice on spiritual matters? How can a believer possibly be edified by the philosophical wanderings of an infidel? How can the living Body of Christ find any merit in the idolatrous practices of superstition and man-made religion?"

The apostle's advice is till this day as sound as it was when he wrote it. God demands that His Blessed Man "come out from among them [the ungodly]" and be separated unto Him. This is positive separation as well as negative separation, and it is blessed separation.

When a man wants advice concerning his automobile, he goes to an automotive mechanic. If a man is wise and needs medical advice, he goes to a good, reputable medical doctor. If a man is in the process of building a house and needs advice on some phase of construction, he goes to an architect or contractor or carpenter, depending upon the exact area of his need. Does it not also make good sense that if a man needs advice on spiritual matters, matters that involve eternity as well as time and space, that he go to someone who is spiritually mature and skilled? It certainly does! Education cannot be an adequate substitute for scriptural spirituality. No amount of worldly wisdom can suffice to answer the questions that arise within the souls of God's children. Therefore, the Blessed Man must have counselors who are born-again men and men who are students of the Word of God.

First, then, *counselors should be men of scriptural principles.* This is very evident from what the apostle Paul says in 1 Corinthians 2:14: "But the natural man receiveth not the things of the Spirit of God: for they are foolishness unto him: neither can he know them, because they are spiritually discerned." Spiritual wisdom can only come from men who are spiritually alive. Men who have been born again are alive to the voice of the Holy Spirit. Again, this is the emphasis of the apostle Paul in 1 Corinthians 2:9 and 10.

> Eye hath not seen, nor ear heard, neither have entered into the heart of man, the things which God hath prepared for them that love him.
> But God hath revealed them unto us by his Spirit:

for the Spirit searcheth all things, yea, the deep things
of God.

Paul says that the natural man has no idea what God
has prepared for His children, BUT "God has revealed
them unto US." The children of God are taught of the Holy
Spirit things which the world has never even dreamed
about. It is the Holy Spirit who teaches us from His Word
"that the man of God may be perfect, throughly furnished
unto all good works" (2 Tim. 3:17).

Not only is this true, but we are also told that the Lord
Jesus Christ Himself is "made unto us wisdom" (1 Cor.
1:30). Having this infinite wisdom at our disposal, we need
not go to worldly, ungodly, self-appointed experts for our
counsel. The Blessed Man walks in the counsel of God-
fearing, Christ-honoring, Bible-believing, born-again men
whose wisdom stems from God Himself.

The prophet Amos poses a very pertinent question in
connection with this line of thinking: "Can two walk together, except they be agreed?" (Amos 3:3). Spiritual counsel should come from men who believe the Bible to be the
Word of God, whose allegiance is to the virgin-born Son of
God and whose desire is that "your faith should not stand
in the wisdom of men, but in the power of God" (1 Cor.
2:5).

James contrasts the difference between worldly wisdom and heavenly wisdom when he writes that the wisdom which is not from above is "earthly, sensual,
devilish." "But the wisdom that is from above is first pure,
then peaceable, gentle, and easy to be intreated, full of
mercy and good fruits, without partiality, and without
hypocrisy" (James 3:15,17). James implies the need for
separation when he states that heavenly wisdom is *first*
pure, *then* peaceable.

The apostle Paul advised young Timothy with reference to this matter of consultation. He wrote:

O Timothy, keep that which is committed to thy
trust, avoiding profane and vain babblings, and oppo-
sitions of science falsely so called:

Which some professing have erred concerning the faith (1 Tim. 6:20, 21).

What Paul here wrote is certainly in perfect agreement with what the psalmist penned.

Second, *counselors should be men of sensible practicality.* The Bible is the most practical book in existence. The Lord Jesus Christ lived the most practical and useful life ever lived. The Christian life when lived according to the will of God is a practical life. There is little room for ivory towers when one is serving Christ.

The Pharisees were most impractical. They had substituted their traditions for the Word of God. They stressed pomp and ceremony and ritualism but cared little about the poverty-stricken, disease-ridden, heartbroken masses of people around them. The Lord Jesus Christ was so different from these religious hypocrites. Christ came to minister! He came as a Servant. He said, "If any man will come after me, let him deny himself, and take up his cross daily, and follow me" (Luke 9:23). The Lord knew that perishing people need more than platitudes.

Christians should seek advice and counsel from men who are practical. Men who are diligently serving the Lord Jesus Christ are men who know life. When we say we should be practical, we do not mean that we should simply do the thing that is expedient. Many times the expedient thing is not always the practical. One should never sacrifice permanent principles upon the altar of present expediency. The philosophy which says "the end justifies the means" is not a scriptural philosophy, and it is certainly not a spiritually practical philosophy.

On the other hand, we believers need not make a task difficult just for the sake of difficulty and hardship. It is not wrong to employ new methods in the service of the King of kings. The Lord Jesus Christ should have our best. Our talents should be developed to the greatest possible degree. Our time should be utilized wisely. Our financial resources ought to be cared for in the most careful manner. The Lord Jesus Christ said that "the children of this world are in their generation wiser than the children of light" (Luke 16:8). In Matthew 10:16 the Lord gave this advice to His disciples: "Behold, I send you forth as sheep in the midst of wolves: be ye therefore wise as serpents, and harmless as doves." In our generation we have many new devices and media by which to preach the gospel. Movie projectors, slide projectors, audiovisual aids, television and radio are devices which should be employed in the spreading of the Good News of the gospel. Wise spiritual counselors will see the wisdom in putting to use every available tool to the glory of the Lord Jesus Christ.

In the history of Israel there is a classic example of a man who did not have enough sense to take the advice of practical men. King Rehoboam had just succeeded Solomon to the throne. Israel had lived in the splendor of Solomon's glory for forty years. Other nations were awed at the wealth and magnificence of Solomon's court. But all of this had cost the common people a great deal. Under Solomon's rule the taxation of the people had become almost unbearable. When Rehoboam took the throne, a delegation headed by Jeroboam came to the new king and asked him to lighten the load of taxation. They said: "Thy father made our yoke grievous: now therefore make thou the grievous service of thy father, and his heavy yoke which he put upon us, lighter, and we will serve thee" (1 Kings 12:4). King Rehoboam asked that he be given three days to consult with his advisors before giving an answer. The king first talked with the old men who had been Solomon's advisors. These men were wise and had no doubt learned much from Solomon. They knew the secrets of Solomon's success. They also knew the reasons for Solomon's decline during the latter years of his life. These men were practical and experienced and wise. They advised the new king to hearken to the people.

But King Rehoboam was not satisfied. The Bible says that "he forsook the counsel of the old men, which they had given him, and consulted with the young men that were grown up with him, and which stood before him" (12:8). When the people came to see Rehoboam at the end of the three-day waiting period, he "answered the people roughly, and forsook the old men's counsel that they gave him" (12:13). The result? The kingdom was split! King Rehoboam was not a practical man, and he would not listen to practical advice.

A New Testament example of a man who refused to take good, practical advice is found in Acts 27. Paul the apostle was on his way by ship to Rome. After a rather rough voyage, the ship came to a place called Fair Havens. Here the apostle advised the centurion with these words: "Sirs, I perceive that this voyage will be with hurt and much damage, not only of the lading and ship, but also of our lives" (27:10). This was practical advice. Paul was of the well-based opinion that to continue the voyage under the circumstances then prevalent would be disastrous. But the centurion was more concerned about his physical comfort and would not heed. So we read: "Because the haven was not commodious to winter in, the more part advised to depart thence also, if by any means they might attain to Phenice, and there to winter" (27:12). The centurion and his advisors wanted to do the expedient thing even when practical common sense advised against it. The result? A ship wrecked, and a total loss of all cargo, and a three-month stay on an island called Melita, a place that probably was not nearly as comfortable as was Fair Havens! Blessed is the man who walks in the counsel of men who are sensibly practical.

Third, *counselors should be men of sound purpose.* Men who advise believers must always be men whose purposes are in line with God's purposes. Bible-believing Christians are not wise to look to political leaders for advice on spiritual and moral matters, for the purposes of these men are not often, generally speaking, the purposes of Bible-believers. Generally, it is the purpose of international politicians to bring about a world of unity and peace in which all evil will somehow be erased and men will live in good will. They talk of a world in which Christian ideals are practiced by all men. Their purpose is to reform society, and they proceed upon the premise that mankind can be made over and society can be changed by education, sanitation and culture.

But is this noble-sounding goal God's purpose for the Church? James says it is not! "Simeon hath declared how God at the first did visit the Gentiles, to take out of them a people for his name" (Acts 15:14). This is the purpose of God in this dispensation of grace — to take out of this world "a people for his name." The business of the Church, the Body of Christ, is not to reform the world, but to preach the gospel to the world.

The Scriptures hold out no hope that the world will get better and better under the influence of the Church. On the contrary, the Bible teaches that the world will gradually get worse, that in the last days "evil men and seducers shall wax worse and worse, deceiving, and being deceived" (2 Tim. 3:13). Bible-believing Christians entertain no illusions that this world will know real peace until the Prince of Peace, Jesus Christ, sits on the throne of David in Jerusalem as King of kings and Lord of lords. Our responsibility, therefore, is to proclaim the gospel of grace until the Savior comes back in mighty cataclysmic power to take over the command of the world. When He sets up His millennial kingdom, then and only then will there be universal peace.

Thus it is that political visionaries are dreaming of that which is entirely out of line with God's purposes. We believers need to be on guard lest we be sidetracked onto tangents that will dissipate our resources and talents. The Blessed Man must have as his advisors those who are sound in purpose or he may get advice that will lead him astray and cause him to waste much precious time and energy.

Sound purposes include these: (1) a desire to exalt the crucified and resurrected Son of God, Jesus Christ, as the only Savior from sin; (2) a determination to honor the Bible as the Word of God, verbally inspired, inerrant and infallible; (3) a determination to keep the testimony of the local church pure; (4) a desire to evangelize the unsaved without compromising the precious convictions which make up "the faith once delivered unto the saints"; (5) a determination to live a life that is victorious over "the lust of the flesh, and the lust of the eyes, and the pride of life."

The apostle Peter describes our distinct position in 1 Peter 2:9: "But ye are a chosen generation, a royal priesthood, an holy nation, a peculiar people; that ye should shew forth the praises of him who hath called you out of darkness into his marvellous light." Blessed is the man whose counselors have sound purposes like these. "Set your affection on things above, not on things on the earth," and make sure your advisors have done the same thing! We need blessed separation from worldly wisdom and political dreaming when it comes to this business of counsel on spiritual matters.

II. Blessed Because of His Conviction

"Blessed is the man that . . . standeth [not] in the way of sinners." The Blessed Man stands with true conviction. His affirmations are scriptural. He has obeyed the command of Paul as given in Ephesians 6:11, 13 and 14:

> Put on the whole armour of God, that ye may be able to stand against the wiles of the devil. . . .
> Wherefore take unto you the whole armour of God, that ye may be able to withstand in the evil day, and having done all, to stand.
> Stand therefore, having your loins girt about with truth, and having on the breastplate of righteousness.

Too many Christians sing "Stand Up for Jesus" but in reality they "Sit Down for the Devil." They sing "Sound the Battle Cry," but they too often cry at the sound of battle. The Blessed Man is one who takes a stand with the right people on the right issues. He stands for Christ and against the Devil. He stands for righteousness and against sin. He stands for the truth and against the lie. Like Joshua of old, he says, " . . . Choose you this day whom ye will serve . . . but as for me and my house, we will serve the LORD" (Josh. 24:15). Like Elijah of long ago, he declares: "How long halt ye between two opinions? if the LORD be God, follow him: but if Baal, then follow him" (1 Kings 18:21). Take your stand!

Oh, for men of conviction! How we need men today who believe the Word of God and whose convictions are well established in the Word of God! We need men like the apostle Paul whose convictions meant more to him than position or comfort or even life itself. Paul wrote: "Yea doubtless, and I count all things but loss for the excellency of the knowledge of Christ Jesus my Lord: for whom I have suffered the loss of all things, and do count them but dung, that I may win Christ" (Phil. 3:8).

We need men like John Hus whose devotion to the truth of God's Word demanded that he stand, even if it meant standing at a stake to burn. And it did mean just that! But he stood, and today the truths for which he stood are still blazing their way into the hearts of men around the globe, though the flames which consumed Hus' mortal body have long since been quenched. Hus refused to stand with the sinful mob of religious dictators of his day, and Hus can be truly classified with God's Blessed Men.

We need men today who have the courage of their convictions, such as Martin Luther. He challenged the religious error of his day with the infallible and eternal truth of the Word of God. Luther's 95 Theses, nailed to the door of the Wittenburg church at midday on October 31, 1517, have become famous. Note what Luther declared in two of these theses. Thesis 92: "Would that we were quit of those preachers who cry to the church, Peace, peace, and there is no peace." In Thesis 94 Luther wrote: "We should exhort Christians to diligence in following Christ their head, through crosses, death, and hell." In other words, Luther was prepared to stand by his convictions regardless of the consequences. His loyalty to Christ and the Word of God would not allow him to "stand in the way of sinners" even though those sinners wore the respectable robes of priesthood.

Only men with such conviction and courage empowered by the Holy Spirit can do a lasting work for God. Compromising men may attract the "truth-seekers" and be applauded by the self-righteous Christ-rejectors, but only men of the caliber of conviction that marked Paul, Hus and Luther do a lasting work for God. The world may not take note of their work, but God does. It may not be recorded in the newspapers of the world, but be assured that God keeps accurate records. The martyrs lost their lives, but they did not lose the battle. Their mouths were stopped, but the truths they taught were given a powerful impetus by the very fact that their proclaimers were willing to die for those truths.

Can you imagine John Hus sugarcoating his Sunday morning sermon so as not to offend a leading member of his congregation who happened to be a big giver? Can you imagine Hus sitting in his study on Saturday night carefully deleting any references in his sermon about sin because those references might offend some snooty-nosed society woman who liked to play cards or suck cigarettes? Of course not! Can you imagine Martin Luther in a deacons' meeting saying to the deacons in an apologetic, wishy-washy tone: "Gentlemen, I am sorry if I offended your feelings last Sunday morning. If you'll just give me one more chance, I'll prove to you that I really am broad-minded and bighearted." Can you imagine Luther doing that? Not on your life! To these men, preaching the Word of God was not a career; it was a holy calling. Preaching, to them, was not a profession; it was a passion. They did not suit their message to please the people to whom they preached; they preached to please God, and that kind of preaching soon suits the right kind of people, and the other kind cannot be pleased anyway!

You cannot win the world by coming down to its standards. You cannot stand in the way of sinners and expect those sinners to respect your message. The Blessed Man knows that standing for the Word of God will automatically offend some people. He knows that when one stands for the truth, a blessed separation occurs, and the worldly crowd will drop the Blessed Man like a hot potato.

Paul wrote to Timothy, "Preach the Word!" We need men today whose hearts will cry, "Woe is unto me, if I preach not the gospel!" The acid of agnosticism can only be dissolved by the preaching of the precious blood of Christ. The brazen betrayal of Bible Christianity called Barthianism can be exposed by the clear proclamation of the verbal plenary inspiration of the Bible. The calloused consciences of hardened sinners can be shaken by declaring the truth of the Lake of Fire. The devilish doctrines spawned by Darwinism can be contradicted by the faithful teaching of the direct creation of man by God. The false fantasies of so-called Christian Science can be exploded by an uncompromising presentation of the profound truths in Romans 5:12: "Wherefore, as by one man sin entered into the world, and death by sin; and so death passed upon all men, for that all have sinned." All of the insidious philosophies of Satan can be overcome by the preaching of the unadulterated Word of God.

Preach the Word! Have convictions based solidly in the Word! Stand in the way of the godly! Refuse to water down your message! Blessed is the man who depends on "Thus saith the Lord." Paul's testimony as a preacher was this: "And my speech and my preaching was not with enticing words of man's wisdom, but in demonstration of the Spirit and of power" (1 Cor. 2:4). Such preaching made the ruler Felix tremble (Acts 24:24, 25).

Daniel was a man of conviction. Daniel was a cultured man and a well-educated man. He was no doubt a very personable individual and a man of leadership. But Daniel was first and foremost a true Israelite. He believed in the God of Abraham, Isaac and Jacob. Daniel's convictions were grounded in the Mosaic Law, and Daniel believed the Word of God. Daniel did not believe in the philosophy, "When in Rome (or Babylon), do as the Romans do." We read in Daniel 1:8: "But Daniel purposed in his heart that he would not defile himself with the portion of the king's meat, nor with the wine which he drank: therefore he requested of the prince of the eunuchs that he might not defile himself." Daniel was a gentleman; he was courteous. But he was unflinchingly firm.

In Daniel 3 we read of three of Daniel's friends who

were also men of conviction and courage. These men—
Shadrach, Meshach and Abednego — worshiped the one
true God. The king, Nebuchadnezzar, made a golden
image which he felt everyone ought to worship. But these
three Hebrew children knew better than to bow to an
image of gold. When the signal was given to bow, these
three men simply did not bow. They not only professed
convictions; they practiced those convictions.

Refusal to obey the king's outrageous command
meant that the three courageous Hebrews would have to
be cast into a fiery furnace, but the God Whose will they
had obeyed saw them safely through the fire. If God can
find men of conviction, He will see these men through any
kind of difficulties that may come until their job is done.
The Romans beheaded Paul but not until his job had been
completed and his course had been finished.

Moses was also a mighty man of conviction. Moses
could have stifled the voice of conscience and lived a life
of ease in the Egyptian lounges of pleasure, but Moses was
made of sterner material. If any man could have had what
most men want, Moses could have. He had been reared in
royal style, and the world was at his feet. He was now at
the crossroads as a young man, and the writer of Hebrews
records Moses' decisive choice for time and eternity in
these words:

> By faith Moses, when he was come to years, re-
> fused to be called the son of Pharaoh's daughter;
> Choosing rather to suffer affliction with the
> people of God, than to enjoy the pleasures of sin for a
> season;
> Esteeming the reproach of Christ greater riches
> than the treasures in Egypt: for he had respect unto
> the recompence of the reward (Heb. 11:24-26).

Moses refused to "stand in the way of sinners" even
though those sinners wore regal robes and lived in palatial,
pleasure-filled mansions. Moses saw past the fleeting pleasures of time. Moses saw the eternal. Moses knew that

Egypt's glory would someday wane and perish. Knowing this, Moses also knew that "he that doeth the will of God abideth for ever." With such conviction, Moses took his stand with God's Chosen People, and history attests to the fact that Moses made the right choice, and the writer of Hebrews surely casts Moses in the role of one of God's Blessed Men.

Yes, a Blessed Man must stand. He must stand for the truth and with the truth, and this means he cannot and will not "stand in the way of sinners."

III. Blessed Because of His Companionship

"Blessed is the man that . . . sitteth [not] in the seat of the scornful." The statement, "Birds of a feather flock together," is more than a trite saying. An individual marks himself by the type of company which he enjoys and seeks out. A professing Christian who desires the company of the worldly crowds belies his profession.

The apostle Paul warns: "Be not deceived: evil communications corrupt good manners" (1 Cor. 15:33). This verse could also be translated, "Bad company ruins good morals." The Blessed Man keeps good company. It is my conviction that Christian people ought to have their closest and dearest friends among God's people. It is best when believers have their choicest friends among the members of their own local church. Fellowship is an important part of the Christian life, and Christians ought to have companions whose lives are an encouragement to godliness.

Of whom is the psalmist speaking when he talks of scorners? Who are these people that we are to avoid? Let us look at "the scornful" from three different angles. First, the *scorners defined*. Webster defines the word *scorn* in its use as a transitive verb in this manner: "To treat with extreme contempt; to mock; deride." This definition is backed up by the Bible's own definition of scornful men. Isaiah gives us this definition as he describes God's coming judgment upon the wicked rulers of Jerusalem:

> · Wherefore hear the word of the LORD, ye scorn-
> ful men, that rule this people which is in Jerusalem.
> Because ye have said, We have made a covenant
> with death, and with hell are we at agreement; when
> the overflowing scourge shall pass through, it shall
> not come unto us: for we have made lies our refuge,
> and under falsehood have we hid ourselves:
> Therefore thus saith the Lord GOD, . . .
> Judgment also will I lay to the line . . . (Isa.
> 28:14-17).

Isaiah's definition of these scornful men, along with Webster's definition, makes clear the following: (1) scorn-ers have a contempt for God's Word and His authority in general; (2) scorners mock at sin and its consequences. "Fools make a mock at sin" (Prov. 14:9); (3) scorners de-ride the thought of judgment; (4) scorners delight in deceit. In short, scorners are vain, pleasure-mad, self-centered, worldly individuals who live for the present and whose phi-losophy is "eat, drink and be merry, for tomorrow may not come." These are the kind of people a wise man will stay away from as much as possible. The Blessed Man will not find his companionship among such people.

Now let us see the *scorners described*. The psalmist tells us that the scornful are "at ease." "Our soul is exceed-ingly filled with the scorning of those that are at ease, and with the contempt of the proud" (Ps. 123:4).

The Book of Proverbs has much to say about the scorn-ful. "A scorner seeketh wisdom, and findeth it not . . ." (14:6). The New Testament counterpart of this proverb is 2 Timothy 3:7, where Paul is describing the scorners of the last days. He says that they are "ever learning, and never able to come to the knowledge of the truth." In scorning the Savior they have scorned the Truth, for He is the Truth. Thus a scorner is correctly described as a vain truth-seeker. Moreover, "A scorner loveth not one that reproveth him . . ." (Prov. 15:12). The sinners in this generation are no different from those of past days. Sinners today do not like their sins exposed from the pulpit any more than Herod appreciated John the Baptist's sermon on the wickedness of wife-stealing and adultery. Preachers today who are faithful in denouncing sin are branded as "sowers of discord" and "apostles of hate." So they, the preachers of righteousness, have always been branded. Elijah was accused by Ahab of "troubling Israel." Jeremiah was called a prophet of doom.

Scorners never appreciate reproof, and their only defense is vituperative mudslinging at the reprovers. "Cast out the scorner, and contention shall go out; yea, strife and reproach shall cease" (Prov. 22:10). In this verse we are told that the actual cause of contention is not the faithful man but the scorner.

Russia's leaders are quite fond of calling the Americans warmongers. But we know better. We do not want war, but neither do we wish to give up all of our precious freedoms just to appease the greed of atheistic communism. Freedom and peace-loving Americans will fight on the battlefields of the world, not because they love to fight but because ungodly aggressors have made it necessary to fight if freedom is to be kept and preserved. So it is in the spiritual realm. The Devil would have us accept peace on his terms. Infidelity asks truth to surrender her tenets for the sake of peace, but the infidel scorners have produced the contention. Thus Paul exhorts us to "fight the good fight of faith."

Paul also describes scorners. The description which Paul gives of men as they shall be in "the last days" certainly sounds like men whom we have described as "scorners." Paul writes: "Men shall be lovers of their own selves, covetous, boasters, proud, blasphemers, disobedient to parents, unthankful, unholy . . . lovers of pleasures more than lovers of God" (2 Tim. 3:2-4). If the Blessed Man of today is in imminent danger of any one peril, it is the peril of pleasure. The United States of America can be rightly described as a pleasure-mad nation. Even many Christians have been swept along in this frenzy for pleasure. It used to be "Sweet Hour of Prayer"; now it is "Special Hour of Television." It used to be "Take Time To Be Holy"; now it is "Take Time To Go Bowling." Many churches are more interested in recreation than they are in revelation. This is tragic, and the Blessed Man must not allow himself to become engrossed in a mad circle of pleasure-mad, time-consuming merry-go-rounds when there is so much to do for the Lord Jesus Christ.

In 1977 the American people reportedly spent *$20 billion* for AMUSEMENTS but only *$200 million* for MISSIONS! Is not this indicative of the plight of a so-called Christian nation? While the world's millions are lost and dying in sin, too, too many Christians are doing nothing more than just dwindling away their time with silly amusements. Instead of spending time in blessed fellowship with other believers at the throne of grace, thousands upon thousands of Christians do not even go to prayer meeting because their favorite TV show is more important to them! Said Paul to idle believers of his day: "Awake to righteousness, and sin not; for some have not the knowledge of God: I speak this to your shame" (1 Cor. 15:34). Blessed is the man who does not sit in the seat of the scornful, pleasure-mad throng of these last days.

Finally, let us listen to the *scorners denounced*. The psalmist declares in Psalm 26:3-5: " . . . I have walked in thy truth. I have not sat with vain persons, neither will I go in with dissemblers. I have hated the congregation of evil doers; and will not sit with the wicked." This is the testimony of the Blessed Man, a man whose loyalty to the Lord makes it impossible for him to consort with the enemies of his Lord. A blessing upon those who are willing to separate themselves from the scornful is also given in Psalm 40:4: "Blessed is that man that maketh the LORD his trust, and respecteth not the proud, nor such as turn aside to lies." In this twentieth century many many false teachers have turned aside to lies. Religious lies, philosophical lies, political lies and sociological lies abound in the teachings of men today. Are we to give Christian recognition to these false teachers simply because they wear a religious halo or give forth an aura of intellectuality? Absolutely not! We have no reason to be ashamed of the simplicity of the gospel of Christ. Neither do we have any reason to respect the perverted scholarship of men whose minds rebelliously refuse to submit to the infallible Word of God. Paul assures us that "the foolishness of God is wiser than men; and the weakness of God is stronger than men" (1 Cor. 1:25). The apostle set the standard when he wrote: "Have no fellowship with the unfruitful works of darkness, but rather reprove them" (Eph. 5:11).

If a man is to be blessed of God, he must be careful to be in the company of God's people often and regularly. Is not this the reason the writer of Hebrews was so emphatic in his plea to the believers of his day?

> And let us consider one another to provoke unto love and to good works:
> Not forsaking the assembling of ourselves together, as the manner of some is; but exhorting one another: and so much the more, as ye see the day approaching (Heb. 10:24, 25).

The Blessed Man, then, in summary, is one who knows the value of blessed separation. He does not walk in the counsel of the ungodly, but his advisors are sound in the faith. He does not stand in the way of sinners; rather, his convictions are unflinchingly true to the Word of God. He does not sit in the seat of the scornful, but his companions are other believers who are actively at work in the service of the Lord Jesus Christ.

Are you willing to live the life of blessed separation? Have you separated yourself from the worldly and sinful practices that characterized your life before you were converted? Remember, "If any man be in Christ, he is a new creature: old things are passed away; behold, all things are become new" (2 Cor. 5:17). As a born-again child of God, you have an obligation to God to walk only in the counsel of true-to-the-Bible ministers and teachers of the gospel. You have a responsibility to stand in the paths of righteousness with others of God's people whose beliefs are true to the Word of God. And you have the happy duty to associate yourself with God's people who will strengthen your faith and encourage your Christian growth.

BLESSED STUDY

I.   His Thirst for Study

    A. Stems from his delight in the Son of God

    B. Stems from his desire to know the will of God

    C. Stems from his determination to overcome sin

    D. Stems from his devotion to the work of soul winning

    E. Stems from his dreams for the future

II. His Textbook for Study

    A. A survey of the Bible

    B. A satisfaction through the Bible

    C. A sword that is two-edged

III. His Tenacity in Study

    A. Submissive meditation

    B. Scripture memorization

    C. Spiritual ministry

CHAPTER TWO

Blessed Study

"But his delight is in the law of the LORD;
and in his law doth he meditate day and
night" (Ps. 1:2).

THE GREAT Roman historian Tacitus described life in Rome under Emperor Domitian in these words: "The charm of indolence creeps over the mind, and we end by loving the inaction which at first we detested." Physical inaction is dangerous; mental idleness is disastrous. Liberalism, the cults and materialism have all made mighty inroads into the Church of Jesus Christ because God's people have been woefully slack in obeying Peter's injunction to "gird up the loins of your mind" (1 Pet. 1:13). Too many Christians who "ought to be teachers . . . have need that one teach" them "the first principles of the oracles of God; and are become such as have need of milk, and not of strong meat" (Heb. 5:12). The psalmist tells us that the Blessed Man is a man of mental activity. He knows the reality of "bringing into captivity every thought to the obedience of Christ." The Blessed Man is aware that what one studies and meditates upon is the ruling force in his life. If you would be blessed of God, "be not conformed to this world: but be ye transformed by the renewing of your mind, that ye may prove what is that good, and acceptable, and perfect, will of God" (Rom. 12:2).

How one studies and what one studies is of the highest importance. Johann Gutenberg studied the possibilities of movable type and gave to the world the printing press, an invention which has been used for more good and at the same time for more evil than probably any device ever known to man. Thomas Jefferson studied political science and human government, and he, with other studious and active early Americans, gave to us a Declaration of Independence and a Constitution which have been the very foundation stones of the greatest and freest nation in the world's history. Sir Humphrey Davy studied the effects of nitrous oxide gas on people who inhaled it, and Sir Humphrey gave to the world its first reliable anesthetic, a discovery which has relieved the sufferings of untold thousands of people. Elisha G. Otis studied steam engines and then invented a steam-powered elevator with a safety brake. In doing so, Mr. Otis has saved us millions of steps and has made skyscraper office buildings a practical reality. Thomas Edison studied electricity and gave the world new beauty, new sounds and new conveniences. Henry Ford studied mechanics and gave the world the automobile. Karl Marx studied economics and history, and he unleashed upon the world the bloody and destructive bear of atheistic communism. Samuel Adams also studied history and economics, but his study produced brilliantly written pamphlets which paved the way for the American Revolution and helped to give a mighty impetus to capitalism. The Wright brothers studied the fascinating ways of the wind and the laws of the air currents, and they gave to the world air travel which has revolutionized warfare as well as transportation habits. Dr. William Coolidge studied the potential usefulness of a hot-cathode X-ray tube and gave to the world a machine which has been of inestimable value in the diagnosis and treatment of disease. Albert Einstein studied the mysteries of science and mathematics and gave to the world the theory of relativity and the atom bomb. Jonas Salk studied medicine and gave the world a vaccine that halted the march of crippling polio.

Indeed, how important is study! Its influence may be

felt across continents. Its impact may jar nations. Its power may mold the habits of millions of people. To study is to strive. To study is to struggle. To study is to climb toward supremacy. This is eminently true in the realm of the spiritual. The Word of God is a fathomless reservoir of knowledge and wisdom and power. The psalmist gave himself to the study of the Word of God, and his life was a blessed one. Moreover, his life was a blessing to many others. In an age when people are so anxious to be doing something, we need to realize that depth of soul can only be attained in the quiet place alone with God. "Be still, and know that I am God," says the Almighty One. The Lord Jesus Christ commended Mary over Martha because Mary sought the place of meditation and study at the feet of her Lord, while Martha was busy about many things which really did not matter so much after all.

The Blessed Man is one who knows the treasures to be had from the toil of thinking. To him, Bible study is not only a responsibility and a duty, it is a wonderful privilege.

I. His Thirst for Study

"But his *delight* is in the law of the LORD." This indicates to us the thirst which this man had for the Word of God. It is no wonder that in another psalm he prays, "O God, thou art my God; early will I seek thee: my soul thirsteth for thee, my flesh longeth for thee in a dry and thirsty land, where no water is" (Ps. 63:1). How we need more God-thirsty men and women today! Many want to be entertained, others want to be active, but few want to know God. Because the psalmist wanted to know God, he loved to study the Word of God.

A man who has come to know the Lord Jesus Christ as his personal Savior needs to cultivate a taste for Bible study. Peter wrote: "As newborn babes, desire the sincere milk of the word, that ye may grow thereby: If so be ye have tasted that the Lord is gracious" (1 Pet. 2:2, 3). The believer's desire to study the Bible grows out of a longing to know better the Lord Jesus Christ, to understand more fully the will of God for daily living, to appropriate more consistently the power of God over sin and the world, to be more effective in the work of soul winning and Christian service, and to be aware of prophetical events yet to occur.

First, the believer's desire to study the Bible stems from a Spirit-implanted desire to know more intimately the Lord Jesus Christ. If you want to learn of Christ, study your Bible. See Him in the Temple as a twelve-year-old lad. Watch Him as He is baptized by John the Baptist. Listen to Him as He proclaims the Sermon on the Mount. Marvel as you watch Him perform mighty miracles. Learn as you sit at His feet and listen to Him teach. Be still and hush your heart as He prays. Grow more aware of His grace as He washes the feet of the disciples in the Upper Room. Wonder at Him as He prays in Gethsemane's Garden. Thank God for Him as He stands in Pilate's judgment hall. Weep over your sin as you see Him hang on Calvary's cross. Rejoice as you hear the angel say, "He is not here: he is risen!" Gaze at Him as He ascends to Heaven. Love Him as you study your Bible. The Bible is the infallible, verbally inspired Word of God, and we must read it reverently and study it submissively if we would come to know our Savior as God wants us to know Him. The Holy Spirit is the Author of the Bible, and it is His purpose to magnify the Son of God to the children of God. The Lord Jesus Christ said: "He [the Holy Spirit] shall glorify me: for he shall receive of mine, and shall shew it unto you" (John 16:14).

Our delight in the Word of God stems from our delight in the Son of God. It is also just as true that our delight in the Son of God stems from our delight in the Word of God. Study your Bible, and you will become acquainted with your Savior. You will learn to love Him and obey Him. Study of the Word of God will bring you to the place where you can say with all of your heart what Bernard of Clairvaux wrote concerning our Savior.

> Jesus, the very thought of Thee
> With sweetness fills my breast;
> But sweeter far Thy face to see
> And in Thy presence rest.

Nor voice can sing, nor heart can frame,
Nor can the mem'ry find
A sweeter sound than Thy blest name,
O Savior of mankind.

O hope of ev'ry contrite heart,
O joy of all the meek,
To those who fall how kind Thou art!
How good to those who seek!

Jesus, our only joy be Thou,
As Thou our prize wilt be;
Jesus, be Thou our glory now
And thru eternity.

The Person and work of Christ can only be learned as one learns his Bible. The Blessed Man will know the Beloved Son through the pages of the Blessed Book.

Second, the believer has a thirst for Bible study because he has a desire to understand more fully the will of God for daily living. In Psalm 37:23 David says, "The steps of a good man are ordered by the LORD. . . ." In Psalm 119:133 he tells us how this is done: "Order my steps in thy word. . . ." The believer needs to study the Bible in order to comprehend the will of God. The Savior said, "Blessed are they which do hunger and thirst after righteousness: for they shall be filled" (Matt. 5:6). No believer has to remain in ignorance as to what the will of the Lord is. Wisdom for day-by-day living is available, and God has placed at our disposal a veritable library of wise instruction for every circumstance of life. The Book of Proverbs alone is inexhaustible in its depth of insight into human nature and daily problems. James tells us that God is happy to meet our request for wisdom. "If any of you lack wisdom, let him ask of God, that giveth to all men liberally, and upbraideth not; and it shall be given him" (James 1:5). Certainly God imparts much wisdom to the one who faithfully and prayerfully studies his Bible. Paul says, "All scripture is given by inspiration of God, and is profitable . . . for instruction in righteousness: That the man of God may be perfect, throughly furnished unto all good works" (2 Tim. 3:16, 17).

A man who desires to know the will of God and is bent on doing that will finds blessing to be his. The Blessed Man is indeed blessed because he has found his "delight" in the "law of the Lord." He knows that the will of God can be found by a diligent and expectant search of the Scriptures. His prayer is found in Psalm 119:169: "Let my cry come near before thee, O LORD: give me understanding according to thy word."

The third reason the believer delights in Bible study is that he wants to appropriate more consistently the power of God over sin and the world. Temptation is a very real thing in every believer's life. Paul, a man familiar with the "good fight of faith," instructs us in this warfare in Ephesians 6. Among many other wonderful "military secrets," he informs us that the Word of God is "the sword of the Spirit." When the Lord Jesus Christ met Satan in the wilderness for personal combat, the Son of God gave us an example as to how to "resist the devil." The Lord Jesus Christ answered Satan's attacking temptations all three times with "thus saith the Lord." Skillfully and certainly the "High Priest of our profession" employed the Sword of the Spirit to the utter dismay of Satan.

You may have victory if you will learn to take the Bible into combat. Again, the psalmist declares, "Thy word have I hid in mine heart, that I might not sin against thee" (Ps. 119:11). In order to be victorious over your foe, you must know the strategy of your foe. You must be acquainted with your enemy's weaknesses and strongpoints. Professional baseball and football teams employ men as scouts. These men are paid above average salaries for one purpose — to find the weak places in the defensive and offensive forces of the opposing teams. It is said that many games are won by the expert information obtained from scouting reports. Let us say reverently but forcefully, we Christians have our scouting reports in the Bible. In 2 Corinthians 2:11, Paul assures his readers that "we are not ignorant of his [Satan's] devices." You can't afford to be ignorant! Satan, "as a roaring lion, walketh about, seeking whom he may devour." Such an avowed enemy must be fought and resisted with supernatural power, and that power is at our disposal! Bible study prepares the believer for battle and equips him for victory in that battle. The writer of Hebrews reminds believers that the Lord Jesus Christ is the "captain of their salvation," and the Captain's orders and battle strategy are in the Bible. If you are to be a good soldier of the Cross, study and obey your Bible. "Onward, Christian Soldiers!" will be a reality in your life and not just a song in the hymnbook if you read and obey the Word of your Commander in Chief.

Believers also study the Bible in order to be more effective in the work of soul winning and Christian service. The work of soul winning is the responsibility of every believer. If you are not endeavoring to win souls, something is wrong with your Bible study. One cannot read far into the New Testament without being confronted with the responsibility to "go ye into all the world, and preach the gospel." Bible study that is not conducive to soul-winning service is not Christ-exalting Bible study. Remember, we said that it is not only important *what* we study but also *how* we study. Marx studied economics and came up with his hideous communism. Samuel Adams studied earlier the history and economics that Marx had studied, but Adams promulgated an entirely different philosophy of life. Why? Each man went at his study from a different perspective.

Some men today study the Bible with proud, self-seeking minds. They judge everything by their brains and intellects. Instead of allowing the infallible Word of God to judge them, they desire to judge the Bible. So-called higher criticism is not reliable since its very foundation rests upon man's "infallible methods of inquiry" while at the same time it refuses to be reverent and submissive in the study of the Bible. The Bible has proved itself to be all that it claims, and it is not subject to the whims and wiles of every new-fangled and modernistic method of intellectual criticism that some self-appointed "Bible scholar" may desire to employ in his "study" of it. How true it is that the Bible is an anvil that has worn out many hammers but is still unbroken itself.

The Bible must be studied submissively and respectfully. It is the Word of God, and the one who reads and studies this Book ought to reverence its Author. Certain it is that men like Voltaire and Ingersoll have long since greatly revised their opinions as to the "mistakes of Moses," etc. No doubt the ribald and mocking slander of these men has long since turned to "weeping and wailing and gnashing of teeth." When one studies the Bible, let him realize that this is no ordinary book. This Book is from God, "God-breathed."

Even some born-again Christians do not study the Bible with the reverence and submissiveness they should. The commands of God are not to be toyed with; they are to be obeyed. Bible study is not for the purpose of increasing our knowledge. That is just a by-product. The believer studies the Bible in order to learn God's will for his everyday life, and most assuredly, that will includes soul winning and service. Too many of God's sheep today are overfed and underworked. They hear good preaching in Bible conferences, in their churches, in their Bible classes, but this study only makes scholars when it should be making servants. Too many people will drive fifty miles to hear about the Battle of Armageddon, but they won't go across the street to battle for their neighbor's soul. Why is this? Is it not because their Bible study has been with the wrong attitude? The Blessed Man delighted in Bible study because Bible study informed him of God's will. Knowing this will, he then went to work to do it. This is God's way of blessing any man or woman. Study your Bible, then put your study into practice!

If you are obediently endeavoring to win souls, you realize how important it is to know the Word of God. This is not to imply that you must have a profound knowledge of the Bible to be a soul-winner. You do not! If you know John 3:16, you can win someone to Christ. But if you are to answer the questions which young Christians will ask, if you are to help those you win to grow in the Lord, then you must be familiar with the Word of God. The more you talk to folks about Christ, the more you will want to study the Bible, because people will ask you questions that will drive you to the Bible for the answers.

If you want to be useful in Christian service, if you want to be used of God to edify other believers, you will have to study the Word. The apostle Paul, whom God used to write half of the New Testament, expressed himself on this subject by saying: "Brethren, I commend you to God, and to the word of his grace, which is able to build you up, and to give you an inheritance among all them which are sanctified" (Acts 20:32). If you will be faithful in your Bible study, God will see to it that you have opportunity to be of help to others. You may have the privilege of teaching a Sunday school class or a young people's group or a Bible study in the home. But be sure that there is always a pre- pared place of service for prepared people.

The final reason we are considering in this particular study as to why believers desire to study the Bible is that of prophecy. All men have some degree of curiosity about the future. Though many unbelievers profess to be uncon- cerned about the hereafter, few of these unbelievers would want to die right now. Why? Because they are not *sure* about the hereafter. Those who have accepted Christ as Savior are certain of eternal life. They may not know what this life may hold for them, but they are sure that when this life ends, eternity will find them with the Lord.

But believers also have a healthy curiosity about the future. The twentieth century has seen a phenomenal growth of interest in the study of prophecy. Prophetic con- ferences are held annually in many churches and schools across the country. The desire to know more of the events surrounding the second coming of Christ makes Bible study a delight to many people. Paul advises us that the grace of God has appeared to us, "teaching us that, denying ungod- liness and worldly lusts, we should live soberly, righ- teously, and godly, in this present world; Looking for that blessed hope, and the glorious appearing of the great God and our Savior Jesus Christ" (Titus 2:12, 13).

The apostle John writes, "And every man that hath this hope in him purifieth himself, even as he is pure" (1 John 3:3). Study of the Word keeps us constantly conscious of the fact that "this same Jesus, which is taken up from you into heaven, shall so come in like manner as ye have seen him go into heaven" (Acts 1:11). As you study the Bible, the truths concerning the pretribulational, premillennial Rapture of the Church will be more precious to you. The blessed hope of the imminent coming of Christ in the air to receive all believers unto Himself makes every day one of obedient "watching" and "occupying."

As you look for Him, you will desire to know more of Him. And as you know more of the King of kings, the greater will be your desire to see Him. Thus, your "delight" will be in "the law of the LORD."

II. His Textbook for Study

Between 1631 and 1645 the Mogul emperor of India, Shah Jahan, built the Taj Mahal, a white alabaster mausoleum. This structure, located at Agra, India, was built as a memorial to the emperor's favorite wife, Mumtaz Mahal. The white alabaster is supposed to be symbolic of this wife's beauty, chastity and purity. Men seem to be quite fond of erecting memorial buildings and shrines. It is sadly true that some Christians treat their Bibles somewhat like Indians treat the Taj Mahal, as a memorial. Having the Bible in the house gives some people the feeling that they are thereby honoring Christ and pleasing God.

But the Bible is *not* a mausoleum! The Bible is not a symbolic memorial to be placed on a parlor table as an exhibit to religious piety! The Bible is the living, dynamic Word of God and is to be read and studied daily. The Blessed Man has one Book that is the center and core of his study — that book is the Bible. His delight is in *the Law of the Lord.*

The pastor's quarters in a church building used to be called the pastor's study. But now his room is known as the pastor's office. This is significant. Pastors used to be men of

God who could say with the first apostles, "We will give ourselves continually to prayer, and to the ministry of the word" (Acts 6:4). The pastor's room was called a study because he spent his time there reading and studying the Word. He invested time in prayer; and when he came to his pulpit, he came with a message from God's throne. But things have changed. The pastor has become a Madison Avenue executive. He is now an administrator who runs a religious corporation (nonprofit, of course), and he spends his time in filing, dictating, conferring and politicking. What does he preach? Oh, he is expert in philosophical discourses on positive thinking or on religious roadways. He can tell you all about the latest in Christian psychology. But his knowledge and use of the Bible are woefully conspicuous by their absence. The Bible has ceased to be his textbook, and his ministry has ceased being blessed of the Lord.

Preacher, listen to the heart cry of the apostle Paul: "Preach *the word;* be instant in season, out of season; reprove, rebuke, exhort with all longsuffering and doctrine" (2 Tim. 4:2). But how can you preach the Word if you don't study it? How can you exhort with all longsuffering and doctrine if you do not know the doctrine? How utterly imperative it is that our textbook be the Bible. All other literature, all other reading should be secondary to the Bible.

Every believer ought to make the Bible an important part of his daily life. Our children need to learn the Bible. Not only is the Bible being left out of many pulpit ministries, but it is also sadly being pushed out of our schools. All kinds of textbooks are being advocated, but the Bible is being allocated to a place of oblivion. It is no wonder that God-fearing parents are more and more seeing the need for Christian day schools and high schools. A man is not truly educated unless he has a knowledge of the Word of God. But the "carnal mind is enmity against God" and desires not to learn or submit to His truth (Rom. 8:7).

Think of all we have in the Bible. A virtual library of knowledge and instruction! Genesis is a course on the beginnings of history and science. Exodus is a travelogue through wilderness trials. Leviticus is a theological illustration book on the holiness of God. Numbers is a study of providential mathematics, while Deuteronomy is a state of the union address by the peerless statesman Moses. Joshua is a course on military strategy. Judges is a bitter lesson in the school of backsliding. Ruth is an introductory survey of courtship and marriage. The books of Samuel make up a course of biography, including the lives of Samuel, Saul and David. The books of Kings are studies in political philosophies as advocated by the kings of Israel and Judah. In Chronicles we are given an illustrated lecture series on the tragedies which befall nations that forget God. Ezra is a treatise on practical theology, while Nehemiah is a seminar on working faith. Esther is a divinely inspired study in applied psychology. Job is an advanced course on the mysteries of suffering and also a vindication of God's infinite wisdom in His dealings with His children. Psalms is an incomparable library of sacred music and poetry.

Proverbs is a book of ethics. Ecclesiastes is a volume of philosophy written by a man of wide experience. Song of Solomon is a beautiful and holy description of love and marriage. Isaiah is a profound study in the Christ-honoring field of prophecy. Jeremiah is a practical course on the preacher and his problems, and this book tells in vivid terms of a man with a message and a heart of compassion that would not compromise his convictions. Lamentations of Jeremiah is a book of warning that what a man sows, he reaps. Ezekiel is an advanced study on Israel's place in the future. Daniel is a tribute to God's faithfulness and a promise of the coming eternal kingdom of the Messiah-King. The Minor Prophets compose a conference on practical living as related to pertinent prophecies. This is the Old Testament, a vast expanse of learning and experience upon which to enrich our souls and our minds.

The New Testament is a Spirit-given seminary course which exalts the Person and work of the Lord Jesus Christ. Matthew presents Him as the fulfillment of Old Testament prophecy. Mark describes His great power. Luke displays

Christ as the perfect Man. John shows Him to be perfect God. Luke teaches the Virgin Birth and shows the fulfillment of Isaiah 9:6a, "For unto us a child is born." John teaches the deity of Christ and also fulfills Isaiah's prophecy, "unto us a son is given," even the everlasting Son of God "which is in the bosom of the Father."

The Book of Acts emphasizes the absolute necessity for the power of the Holy Spirit in the proclamation of the gospel and in the establishing of churches. Romans is a masterful discourse on the great doctrines of salvation, stressing the grace and righteousness of God. The epistles to the Corinthians are a much-needed seminar on church discipline. Galatians is a course on God's grace. Ephesians expounds the truth of the Church, the Body of Christ. Philippians is a course on spiritual fitness. Colossians is a study in Christian apologetics. The epistles to the Thessalonians are an exposition on the second coming of Christ. Paul's epistles to Timothy and Titus give us a study in pastoral relations. Philemon is a masterpiece in pastoral psychology.

The student finds his heart and mind thrilled and challenged thus far. But there is more! Hebrews is a pattern of Christian polemics and proves that the work of the Lord Jesus Christ supercedes as well as fulfills the Law. The work of Christ is all-sufficient for salvation. James could be called the New Testament book of Proverbs, for James accents the practical, everyday life of faith. First Peter exalts the atoning work of Christ. Second Peter warns of the apostasy. It is a tragedy that more seminaries do not likewise warn of the apostasy. The epistles of John are doctrinally practical studies dealing with the believers as a family. First John is a basic study on assurance. Second John warns that only "the truth" is the believer's resource of strength during apostasy. Third John is instruction in righteousness. Jude is a class for contenders for the faith. In this book the apostates are identified and described and God's people are commanded to "earnestly contend for the faith which was once delivered unto the saints." The Book of Revelation is divine drama. The apostle John here teaches an enthralling course on prophecy and the consummation of redemption.

All of this is for your edification and learning! "All scripture is given by inspiration of God, and is profitable for doctrine, for reproof, for correction, for instruction in righteousness: That the man of God may be perfect, throughly furnished unto all good works" (2 Tim. 3:16, 17). What a textbook! And if you would be a Blessed Man, make this Book *your* textbook. The Lord Jesus Christ said, "Whosoever heareth these sayings of mine, and doeth them, I will liken him unto a wise man, which built his house upon a rock" (Matt. 7:24). How we need to build our lives on His Word! The Good Shepherd promises, "I am the way, the truth, and the life: no man cometh unto the Father, but by me" (John 14:6). Here is certainty of leadership, authoritative knowledge and abundance of life. Education seeks a road to satisfaction through the accumulation of knowledge. Materialism labors for a path to happiness by grasping for an abundance of things. Pleasure advertises itself as a lane to luxury. But Jesus says, "I AM THE WAY!"

Agnosticism doubts truth. Rationalism questions truth. Infidelity scoffs at truth. Religion seeks truth. Logic dissects truth. Education talks about truth. But Jesus says, "I AM THE TRUTH!"

Philosophy theorizes about life. Psychology analyzes life. History records life. Science experiments with life. Sociology classifies life. Men desire life. And Jesus says, "I AM THE LIFE!" No wonder it is that he who builds his life on the Word of Christ builds on an eternal Rock.

III. His Tenacity in Study

"And in his law doth he meditate day and night."

In early December 1777, General George Washington arrived in Valley Forge, Pennsylvania, with approximately 11,000 soldiers. Washington's army lacked adequate shelter, clothing, food and medical supplies. The winter of 1777-78 was a cruel one, and it is believed that Washington's army was reduced by some 3,000 men perishing in the icy, bitter weather. Americans are familiar with the story of how Washington and Baron von Steuben rallied the undernourished, discouraged army in February 1778, resulting in the taking of Philadelphia in June of that year. These American soldiers hung on despite overwhelming odds. They did so because they sincerely and intensely believed in the cause of freedom. Their tenacity through trial gave them eventual triumph.

The Blessed Man is one who does not become bored with routine. To a great degree, life is made up of the routine. A newspaper article once told of a girl in a California city who shot her brother. When she was asked why she killed him, she replied, "Oh, I just became bored with doing the same thing around here every day; so I thought I would kill him for some excitement." That is a sad and twisted view of life and death, is it not?

But the Blessed Man finds that even the routines of life can be filled with numberless blessings. He knows that meditation upon the Word of God gives encouragement through the Valley Forge experiences of our spiritual warfare. If we are armed with the Word of God, the chilling winds of worldliness cannot overcome us. The psalmist reveals that the Blessed Man was not only delighted and thrilled to be able to study the Bible, but he was also *consistent* in his study and *constant* in his meditation.

How God desires that we be continually in an attitude of conscious devotion to Him. "Pray without ceasing." "Rejoice evermore." And now we find the psalmist meditating "day and night." Dr. Bob Jones, Sr., often said that all great men have at sometime or other "come under the dominating power of a great truth." If truth is to bless us, it must dominate us. The need today is for Christians who will live consistently for Christ. This business of "mountain-top today and down-in-the-dumps tomorrow" is a sorry affair. Believers need to have spiritual stamina. We need to be "instant in season, out of season." We must learn to "run with patience the race that is set before us." This is a must in our study of the Bible.

The Blessed Man meditates in the Word of God day

and night. Every believer needs a quiet time of communion with the Lord every day. This time will be used in prayer, Bible study and quiet meditation away from the buzzing, milling, rushing world. I believe regular Bible study will do more for spiritual stamina than public services could ever hope to do. Now that is no excuse to stay away from public services! You need all of those you can get too! But public services cannot take the place of private study. Believers need to spend more time studying their Bibles and less time watching the boob tube. Good Christian literature ought to be part of our daily diet. I believe it is good to read through the Bible at least once a year. This keeps one conversant with the whole Bible. Just the reading of three or four chapters a day will ensure you of getting through the Bible every year, and this general reading will be a tremendous background for other more intensive study. As you see the Bible as a whole, the several parts will have even greater significance, and each book will take on a new meaning.

Scripture memorization will also be of profound help to the spiritual stamina of a believer. If you memorize Scripture, then you can meditate upon it. You can think about the words and apply the words to your daily tasks and testimony. Such a program of memorization takes tenacity. It takes a determination that will not be daunted by the changing circumstances of every day. But such determination is worth it! God said to Joshua: "This book of the law shall not depart out of thy mouth; but thou shalt meditate therein day and night, that thou mayest observe to do according to all that is written therein: for then thou shalt make thy way prosperous, and then thou shalt have good success" (Josh. 1:8). Spiritual prosperity? Spiritual success? Yes! How? By obedience to the Word of God which has become a part of you through your systematic, tenacious, day-by-day study of its pages.

"Back to the Bible" should be the cry of individuals, churches and seminaries across this land of ours. Men do not want the polished stones of man's learning; they want the Bread of Life. Men do not need the calculated guesses of other men concerning eternal things; they need the sure word of prophecy. Only the Word of God can meet the needs of hearts. "Behold, the days come, saith the Lord GOD, that I will send a famine in the land, not a famine of bread, nor a thirst for water, but of hearing the words of the LORD" (Amos 8:11). Is this famine raging in your church? in your Sunday school? in your home? in your individual life? Remember, "Man shall not live by bread alone, but by every word that proceedeth out of the mouth of God" (Matt. 4:4).

Who is the Blessed Man? He is one whose "delight is in the law of the LORD; and in his law doth he meditate day and night."

BLESSED STABILITY

I. Planted Properly

    A. A picturesque simile
    B. A proper site
    C. A plentiful supply

II. Producing Perennially

    A. The fruit of the Spirit
    B. The fruit of soul winning
    C. The fruit of stewardship

III. Prospering Prolifically

    A. Long-range prosperity
    B. Wide-range prosperity
    C. Eternal results
    D. Extensive responsibilities

 CHAPTER THREE

Blessed Stability

"And he shall be like a tree planted by the rivers of water, that bringeth forth his fruit in his season; his leaf also shall not wither; and whatsoever he doeth shall prosper"
(Ps. 1:3).

JAMES DECLARES "A double minded man is unstable in all his ways" (James 1:8). The Blessed Man, however, is stable in all his ways since he is single-minded and can say with the apostle Paul, "This one thing I do." The Lord Jesus Christ promised, "If thine eye be single, thy whole body shall be full of light." The man who purposes to do God's will finds delight in learning and obeying that will. Such a man is marked by stability.

Christian singleness of purpose is imperative if the believer is to survive the ungodly forces around him. In Ephesians 4, the apostle Paul explains that the gifts of the ministry were given for the "perfecting of the saints. . . . That we henceforth be no more children, tossed to and fro, and carried about with every wind of doctrine, by the sleight of men, and cunning craftiness, whereby they lie in wait to deceive." The believer has resources of which the world is ignorant. The Blessed Man appropriates these resources and thus answers to the description found in Psalm 1:3.

51

I. Planted Properly

You are not where you are by accident! If you are in the will of God, your life and circumstances are not happenstance. When Joseph revealed himself to his brothers, he said, "Be not grieved . . . that ye sold me hither: for God did send me before you to preserve life. . . . So now it was not you that sent me hither, but God . . ." (Gen. 45:5, 8). Joseph was in Egypt because God planted him there. How blessed to know that one's place in life has been chosen by God! When God does the planting, there is eternal blessedness; but "Every plant, which my heavenly Father hath not planted, shall be rooted up" (Matt. 15:13).

"He shall be like a tree planted by the rivers of water." In considering this statement, we shall proceed along these three lines:

> A. A picturesque simile — "a tree"
> B. A proper site — "planted by the rivers of water"
> C. A plentiful supply — "rivers of water"

The psalmist uses a *picturesque simile* in presenting to us the blessedness of God's man. He shall be like a tree. It was Joyce Kilmer who wrote, "I think that I shall never see a poem lovely as a tree." A tree is an appropriate picture of the believer with respect to endurance, usefulness, fruitfulness, strength and beauty. A tree's ability to stand the storms and winds around it depends upon the depth of its roots. In other words, the secret of its strength is unseen. The tree grows upward as it grows downward. The trunk only becomes massive and strong as the tree's roots go deeply into the soil and ground the tree sufficiently to enable it to take the weight of all that is above the ground. It is certainly true that a believer's outward testimony is only a reflection of his inward and unseen strength.

The difference between a Paul and a Demas is depth of soul. Paul withstood the testings and temptations of the world, for Paul was "rooted and grounded" in Christ. Demas was shallow. Demas looked all right on the surface, but he did not have anything to hold him and ground him when the soft breezes turned to lashing gales. A victorious believer is like a tree in his endurance.

The believer is like a tree in usefulness. How wonderfully useful are trees! In the summertime trees are welcome because they shade from the intense heat of the sun. Have you ever tried to "take the heat off of someone"? A believer can be useful as a shade tree. "Bear ye one another's burdens, and so fulfil the law of Christ" (Gal. 6:2).

A row of trees can also shield one from the wind. We once lived in a home surrounded by trees. There was a row of pine trees in the back of our house and huge sycamore trees in the front. These trees acted as windbreakers. Paul was a windbreaker in behalf of Onesimus. Paul interceded for Onesimus when he wrote to Philemon, "If he hath wronged thee, or oweth thee ought, put that on mine account." Paul's majesty and strength as a "tree" never were more evident than in that statement. Do you know someone for whom you could intercede?

Trees are useful, moreover, as havens of hospitality. Squirrels and many birds would be in desperate straits were it not for the trunks and branches of accommodating trees. Listen to Hebrews 13:1 and 2: "Let brotherly love continue. Be not forgetful to entertain strangers: for thereby some have entertained angels unawares." Paul said that a bishop or pastor must be "given to hospitality." Do people come to you for counsel and advice and comfort? Are you a haven in any respect?

Then, a believer's life is like a tree in the matter of fruitfulness. In Matthew 7:17 and 18 the Savior said: "Even so every good tree bringeth forth good fruit; but a corrupt tree bringeth forth evil fruit. A good tree cannot bring forth evil fruit, neither can a corrupt tree bring forth good fruit." We will have much to say about fruitfulness later in this chapter, but suffice it to say now that a believer's life ought to bear much fruit. Jesus said, "He that abideth in me, and I in him, the same bringeth forth much fruit" (John 15:5).

A tree serves as a fit simile for it is a symbol of strength. A believer ought to be "strong in the Lord, and in the power of his might" (Eph. 6:10). This power is in us because the Holy Spirit dwells within, but we need to yield our members to Him. Our bodies should be presented "a living sacrifice." We are commanded to "be filled with the Spirit." Strength should characterize our testimony, our preaching, our service, our faith and our resisting of the Devil.

Finally, a tree is characteristic of a Christian because of its beauty. Paul told Titus that believers ought to "adorn the doctrine of God our Saviour in all things" (Titus 2:10). The apostle reveals that preachers have beautiful feet! "How beautiful are the feet of them that preach the gospel of peace, and bring glad tidings of good things!" (Rom. 10:15). "The LORD taketh pleasure in his people: he will beautify the meek with salvation" (Ps. 149:4). The life of a believer ought to show forth the beauty of Christ. Grace and truth ought to be evident in our actions and words. The Blessed Man is "like a tree."

Next, let us consider the *proper site*. The Blessed Man is planted by the rivers of water. Take note of the fact that he is *planted*. The Blessed Man is where God wants him. The Lord Jesus Christ said, "My Father is the husbandman," and the Heavenly Father knows exactly where to plant each "tree" of His. God has a prepared place in life for each of us. He has prepared the soil and provided the surroundings so that the tree will prosper properly. Then He *plants* the tree. Paul could say, "I am an apostle by the will of God." God had planted the apostle, and Paul was delighted to be a "bondslave of Jesus Christ."

God's wisdom in placing individuals where they are most needed is an evidence of His omniscience. In 1 Corinthians 12 the apostle Paul expounds on this subject:

> But now hath God set the members every one of them in the body, as it hath pleased him.

And if they were all one member, where were
the body?

But now are they many members, yet but one
body.

And the eye cannot say unto the hand, I have no
need of thee: nor again the head to the feet, I have no
need of you (vv. 18-21).

We need to be submissive and sensitive to the leadership of the Holy Spirit, and we should be able to say with certainty, "I am in this position or calling because God planted me here."

God took Abraham out of Ur of the Chaldees in order to plant him in the land of Palestine. God took Joseph through slavery and imprisonment in order to plant him on a throne in Egypt. God led Moses through the palatial halls of Egypt's kingly mansions, then to the backside of a desert for forty years and finally to a burning bush before He planted Moses in the place of leadership which he occupied for forty years. God carefully cultivated the "sapling" David while David was keeping his father's sheep until the time was ripe for planting David on the throne of Israel where he grew to be a great and blessed tree. Daniel had to walk through a lion's den before he was "rooted and grounded" as mainstay of the king. The Lord Jesus Christ skillfully and wisely prepared the disciples before planting them in their respective places of service. What God may have in store for you, reader, before you find yourself "planted" in the place of His choice may lead you through college halls or hospital rooms or prison cells. But He never errs. D. L. Moody said, "God always gives His best to those who leave the choice with Him."

God knows how to plant you, when to plant you, where to plant you, and why you should be planted. Saul thought David a poor choice to challenge Goliath. But God knew better. If you will delight in the Word of God and obey it, God will plant you properly.

We live in a day when landscaping has become a tremendously important and much-in-demand profession.

Landscapers, nurserymen, tree surgeons are now big businessmen, performing necessary and appreciated tasks. Without their work, many houses would not possess half of the charm which they do. Landscaping which is properly and expertly done can make a lawn or a campus or a hillside beautiful to behold. A tree surgeon who knows the art of pruning as well as planting can transform the atmosphere of a piece of real estate. He knows where to place the shrubs, where to locate the shade trees, how many evergreens to plant. When he gets finished, the property is worth more and possesses a beauty which makes people sit up and take notice.

Reverently speaking, may we suggest that God is the omnipotent tree surgeon. He, with one glance of His eye, can take in the whole landscape of life. He knows what tree is needed where in order to enhance the beauty of His Church. He knows where the shade trees will be most useful, where the evergreens will be most needed. If we will allow Him to "do of his good pleasure" with us, He will plant each of us in the landscape of His will in a place that will honor Him and bless the lives of many many others.

The Blessed Man also has a *plentiful supply*. God always plants His trees by "rivers of living water." What a promise we have in Philippians 4:19: "But my God shall supply all your need according to his riches in glory by Christ Jesus." How could we possibly doubt God's desire to lavish His grace and mercy upon us after His giving to us the Lord Jesus Christ? "He that spared not his own Son, but delivered him up for us all, how shall he not with him also freely give us all things?" (Rom. 8:32).

Trees need nourishment! Trees must have water and sunlight and nourishing soil. The Lord Jesus Christ is the Sun of Righteousness to us. He is also the Water of Life. His Word is our food. In Him we have a beautiful provision. Jesus said, "He that cometh to me shall never hunger; and he that believeth on me shall never thirst" (John 6:35).

But what is meant by "rivers of living water"? The Incarnate Word answers that question in John 7:37-39:

If any man thirst, let him come unto me, and drink.

He that believeth on me, as the scripture hath said, out of his belly shall flow rivers of living water.

(But this spake he of the Spirit, which they that believe on him should receive: for the Holy Ghost was not yet given; because that Jesus was not yet glorified.)

The Holy Spirit is sadly neglected by many of God's people today. He is grossly misrepresented by still others of God's people. But neither extreme is necessary, for the Lord Jesus Christ said, "But when the Comforter is come . . . even the Spirit of truth . . . he shall testify of me" (John 15:26). Our witness for Christ cannot be effective unless that witness is in the power of the Holy Spirit.

We should keep in mind three truths concerning the Holy Spirit's relationship to the experience of the believer. First, every believer has been *baptized in* the Spirit. This truth is found in 1 Corinthians 12:13: "For by one Spirit are we all baptized into one body, whether we be Jews or Gentiles, whether we be bond or free; and have been all made to drink into one Spirit." This is baptism in the Spirit. This baptism took place on the Day of Pentecost as recorded in Acts 2. The entire Body of Christ was represented by that group of believers gathered in the Upper Room, and on the Day of Pentecost every believer was baptized in the Spirit. This is what the apostle Paul refers to in Ephesians 4:5 where he mentions "one baptism." The Pentecostal experience was a once-for-all experience for the Body of Christ. (For a more complete discussion of this, see M. R. DeHaan, *Pentecost and After* [Grand Rapids: Zondervan Publishing House, 1964], pp. 40-44.)

The second important truth we should keep in mind is the *indwelling of* the Spirit in the body of each believer. Paul says in Romans 8:9: "Now if any man have not the Spirit of Christ, he is none of his." When an individual receives Christ as his personal Savior, he experiences the indwelling of the Holy Spirit, Who comes to abide in the body of the believer. The believer is thus experientially made a member of the already baptized Body of Christ.

The third truth concerning the Holy Spirit that is so vital to our daily Christian experience is the *filling with* the Holy Spirit. The baptism and the indwelling have to do with our salvation. The filling with the Spirit has to do with power and effectiveness in serving our Savior. Again, the apostle Paul explains for us: "And be not drunk with wine, wherein is excess; but be filled with the Spirit" (Eph. 5:18).

On the Day of Pentecost the believers were not only baptized in the Spirit; they were also filled with the Spirit. The baptism was a once-for-all experience, since the Holy Spirit was then given to the Body of Christ for this entire dispensation of grace. But the filling with the Spirit can be a repeated experience. We read in Acts 4:31: "And when they had prayed, the place was shaken where they were assembled together; and they were all filled with the Holy Ghost, and they spake the word of God with boldness."

What does it mean to be filled with the Spirit? In Ephesians 5:18 Paul draws a comparison. He says, "Be not drunk with wine." To be drunk with wine is to be controlled by the wine. The power of the wine takes over your faculties. So Paul writes, "But be filled with the Spirit." Allow the Spirit of God to control and use you. This can only be done as we empty ourselves of sin and disbelief and all else that the Word of God reveals to us is displeasing to the Spirit of God. A vessel can only be filled with one substance. The Holy Spirit will not share our hearts with any other worldly or fleshly power. They must go if He is to take over and control us. Note that the Lord Jesus Christ refers to the Spirit with the words "rivers of living water." Don't be drunk or filled with the polluted wines of this world, but be filled with and controlled by the "rivers of living water," even the blessed Holy Spirit. He is God's plentiful supply for every believer.

II. Producing Perennially

The Blessed Man is one "that bringeth forth his fruit in his season." This fruitfulness, of course, is the result of the filling with the Holy Spirit. The Blessed Man is filled with the Spirit, and his life is a blessing "in season and out of season." Or, to put it in the language of the psalmist, the Blessed Man produces his fruit perennially. Webster defines *perennial* with these words: "continuing without cessation or interruption; unceasing; neverfailing." What a description of the fruitfulness of the Blessed Man! Our lives can be unceasingly fruitful if we are filled with the Spirit. What kind of fruit should we produce? Three types of fruits come to our attention in this study.

A. The fruit of the Spirit
B. The fruit of soul winning
C. The fruit of stewardship

In Galatians 5:22 and 23 the apostle Paul writes: "But the fruit of the Spirit is love, joy, peace, longsuffering, gentleness, goodness, faith, Meekness, temperance: against such there is no law." This fruit should be produced in our lives. In Romans 5:5 the apostle tells us that "the love of God is shed abroad in our hearts by the Holy Ghost which is given unto us." The Holy Spirit is responsible for the love of God being "shed abroad in our hearts," and He is also responsible for our joy, peace, long-suffering, gentleness, goodness, faith, meekness and temperance. How tragic it is to see unsaved, unregenerate men and women trying to produce the fruit of the Spirit in their lives. Little do they realize that all of their righteousnesses are as "filthy rags" in the sight of God. (Isa. 64:6). Men try to counterfeit the fruit of the Spirit, but it is impossible for a bad tree to bring forth good fruit. Men may not be able to distinguish between the wheat and the tares, but be sure that God can and will!

The Spirit of God can enable us to love the unlovely, to be joyful amidst suffering, to be peaceful amidst worldly chaos, to be long-suffering through trials, to be gentle when others would be harsh and brutal, to be good in a perverse generation, to have faith when obstacles seem insurmountable, to be meek when the flesh wants to be mean, to be temperate though the world thinks it "strange that ye run not with them to the same excess of riot" (1 Pet. 4:4). Only the Holy Spirit can produce such fruit! Our carnal natures are not capable of it. Our striving cannot accomplish it. Only as we meditate upon the Word of God and send our roots into the "rivers of living water" can we see such fruit produced in our lives. As we study the Bible, we come to know the mind of the Spirit more accurately, and we seek to live so as not to grieve or quench Him. It is the work of the Spirit to glorify the Lord Jesus Christ, and the trees of our lives will be fruitful as we take in the sunshine of the Sun of Righteousness day after day.

The fruit of soul winning should be produced perennially in our lives. Believers ought to reproduce themselves. "The fruit of the righteous is a tree of life; and he that winneth souls is wise" (Prov. 11:30). The Lord Jesus Christ promised: "But ye shall receive power, after that the Holy Ghost is come upon you: and ye shall be witnesses unto me both in Jerusalem, and in all Judaea, and in Samaria, and unto the uttermost part of the earth" (Acts 1:8). The power of the Holy Spirit is given to believers for effective witnessing. Every believer ought to be filled with the Spirit, and every believer ought to win souls.

The psalmist gives a formula for successful witnessing: "He that goeth forth and weepeth, bearing precious seed, shall doubtless come again with rejoicing, bringing his sheaves with him" (Ps. 126:6). What is the formula? First, *the condition* to be met — "going forth." Jesus said, "Go ye." Second, *the compassion* of the soul-winner — "and weepeth." Paul wrote, "I have great heaviness and continual sorrow in my heart . . . for my brethren" (Rom. 9:2, 3). Third, *the cargo* of the soul-winner — "bearing precious seed." Paul says, "Faith cometh by hearing, and hearing by the word of God" (Rom. 10:17). Fourth, *the certainty* of success in soul-winning effort — "shall doubtless come again with rejoicing." Dr. Luke wrote these words concerning the Philippian jailor, who had just accepted Christ as his Savior under the ministry of Paul and

Silas: "And when he had brought them into his house, he set meat before them, and rejoiced, believing in God with all his house" (Acts 16:34). There is always rejoicing when souls are won to the Lord Jesus Christ. Finally, *the conservation* of soul-winning results — "bringing his sheaves with him." Acts 16:5: "And so were the churches established in the faith, and increased in number daily." This, then, is the psalmist's formula for soul winning.

Pastors ought to win souls. Deacons should be active soul-winners. Sunday school teachers should win their pupils to Christ. Parents ought to lead their children to Christ. *Every* believer has the responsibility and privilege of being a soul-winner. It is not the New Testament plan to let the evangelists and pastors do all the soul winning. They could not possibly get the job done by themselves anyway. It is God's plan that every believer be fruitful and multiply himself by faithfully testifying to those around him concerning the saving grace of the Lord Jesus Christ.

Moreover, the fruit of stewardship should be evident in our lives. Perhaps you have never thought of stewardship in relationship to fruitfulness, but I do not believe that a believer who is stingy with his material possessions can be fruitful in his spiritual undertakings. If God touches a heart, He also reaches the man's pocketbook. More than one rich young ruler has gone away from the Lord Jesus Christ in sorrow because, having great riches, he would not give them up to serve the Lord. Poverty is generally thought to be a curse. But prosperity often is a curse. Poverty can sorely try a man. But prosperity can also try a man. Sometimes poverty keeps us more dependent upon God, whereas prosperity tends to make us dangerously self-sufficient.

Paul had learned a great deal in the school of dedication by the time he could write:

> Not that I speak in respect of want: for I have learned, in whatsoever state I am, therewith to be content.
> I know both how to be abased, and I know how to abound: every where and in all things I am in-

structed both to be full and to be hungry, both to abound and to suffer need.
.   I can do all things through Christ which strengtheneth me (Phil. 4:11-13).

The Philippians, to whom Paul wrote those words, were good examples of the fruitfulness of stewardship. Their faithfulness in providing for the material needs of the apostle made it possible for him to do the work of the ministry more effectively and efficiently.

Note the wonderful promise made in Proverbs 3:9 and 10: "Honour the LORD with thy substance, and with the firstfruits of all thine increase: So shall thy barns be filled with plenty, and thy presses shall burst out with new wine." I, as many pastors, have been asked the question, "Shall I tithe my gross or my net income?" To me, that question reveals a lack of joy in giving to the Lord. We should not figure our tithe to the nearest decimal point in order that we do not overdo our giving! Certainly one whose heart is in the work of the gospel is going to see just how much more he can give over 10 percent instead of trying to figure out ways to make the 10 percent less! But to answer the question — the writer of Proverbs tells us to honor the Lord with the firstfruits "of all thine increase." Give a tithe of your gross, and then if you want to know the joy of really giving, give 10 percent more!

Why? Second Corinthians 9:6 gives the answer: "But this I say, He which soweth sparingly shall reap also sparingly; and he which soweth bountifully shall reap also bountifully." If you want to be fruitful, you must sow much seed.

Yes, the Blessed Man "bringeth forth his fruit in his season." He brings forth his fruit perennially. In his life is seen the fruit of the Spirit. He also produces the fruit of winning souls. And he proves his treasure to be in Heaven by being a good steward of what material blessings may be his. All of his fruitfulness depends upon the One Who is our Source of life and nourishment, even the Sun of Righteousness and the Water of Life. He said, "I am the vine, ye are the branches: He that abideth in me, and I in him, the same bringeth forth much fruit: for without me ye can do nothing" (John 15:5). This leads us to our next subject of consideration.

III. Prospering Prolifically

"His leaf also shall not wither; and whatsoever he doeth shall prosper." The psalmist continues his description of the fruitfulness of the Blessed Man with assurance that "his leaf also shall not wither." This is *long-range prosperity.* "Whatsoever he doeth shall prosper." This is *wide-range prosperity.* The Blessed Man is certain of *eternal results* from *extensive responsibilities.* He acts upon and believes Isaiah 32:20: "Blessed are ye that sow beside all waters." He knows that a word spoken for the Lord can bring a greater harvest sometimes than a whole sermon, and he values every opportunity since "redeeming the time" *here* means reward in eternity *hereafter.*

For what does the world live? Men make careful preparations for a career, for retirement, for the education of their children, for hospital bills, but so very few make any preparation for eternity. Men act as though this life will never end. They need to heed the words of the Lord Jesus Christ in Mark 8:36: "For what shall it profit a man, if he shall gain the whole world, and lose his own soul?"

To spend all of one's energies in pursuit of worldly gain is to play the part of a fool. Solomon explains why in Ecclesiastes 2:18 and 19:

> Yea, I hated all my labour which I had taken under the sun: because I should leave it unto the man that shall be after me.
> And who knoweth whether he shall be a wise man or a fool? yet shall he have rule over all my labour wherein I have laboured, and wherein I have shewed myself wise under the sun. This is also vanity.

Solomon was evaluating life from the standpoint of the natural man, and from this standpoint everything of necessity is vanity. If all I am to live for is to someday perish, how vain my life is!

But, thank God, the Christian is not living for time; he is living for eternity! What he does in time has meaning for eternity. The work which he performs, the words which he utters, the thoughts which he activates, all of these are being recorded by the Lord, and reward awaits the faithful servant. The Christian who deals with the souls of men is dealing with eternal merchandise. The believer lives for Christ because he believes that eternal bliss is infinitely more valuable than time-bound thrills and pleasures.

Because Moses had his eye on eternal things, he chose to suffer the reproach of Christ than to "enjoy the pleasures of sin for a season; . . . for he had respect unto the recompence of the reward" (Heb. 11:25, 26). Truly Moses's leaf did not wither. The influences which he put into effect still rule great segments of the world's population today.

Who can tell what mighty influence one dedicated life can wield? Think of the chain of events that was started by the man who witnessed to D. L. Moody. Meditate upon the mighty results of Moody's ministry, but do not forget that man who led Moody to Christ. Do you think your responsibility as a Sundy school teacher is quite unimportant? Do you not have faith to believe that God will not allow your "leaf" to wither? Do you think your seed will not be blessed in time to come and through eternity? Who knows but what another Charles Spurgeon or Hudson Taylor may be listening to your voice in that small, insignificant Sunday school class? Be faithful and be assured that your leaf shall not wither.

The Christian lives for that which lasts! How sad to come to the end of life with the sentiments expressed by Lord Byron in his poem entitled "On This Day I Complete My Thirty-sixth Year." Lord Byron's life was a tempestuous and unhappy one marked by bitterness, disappointments and frustration. Byron's last poem was written just three months before he died in Greece, where he was aiding the Greeks in their battle for independence from the Turkish oppressors. Byron wrote:

My days are in the yellow leaf;
The flowers and fruits of love are gone;
The worm, the canker, and the grief
Are mine alone!

What a tragic contrast to the believer who can triumphantly write, "I have fought a good fight, I have finished my course, I have kept the faith: Henceforth there is laid up for me a crown of righteousness . . ." (2 Tim. 4:7, 8). Paul's leaf has never withered. The life of Paul, that dedicated life, that Christ-centered life, that Spirit-controlled and Spirit-led life, has never stopped bearing fruit down to this twentieth century.

And when you give your heart and life unreservedly to Christ, you can be sure that God will use you in His omniscience to bless other lives until time shall be no more—even after you have gone to be with Him. "The world passeth away, and the lust thereof: but he that doeth the will of God abideth for ever" (1 John 2:17). This is what the writer of Hebrews portrays in that marvelous eleventh chapter, a chapter that is sometimes called the Bible's Hall of Fame. For example, he says of Abel, "By faith Abel offered unto God a more excellent sacrifice than Cain, by which he obtained witness that he was righteous, God testifying of his gifts: and by it he being dead yet speaketh" (Heb. 11:4). The long ages of time have not erased Abel's testimony nor have the rivers of blood which have drenched the battlefields of the world been able to drown his witness. Cain could not still the voice of his brother nor have all of the descendants of Cain and his ilk been able to bury the message of him who "being dead yet speaketh."

Lord Byron wrote as he did because he had realized the folly of sowing to the flesh. Paul wrote as he did because he knew the wisdom of sowing to the Spirit. The Blessed Man's leaf shall not wither because he has been "born again, not of corruptible seed, but of incorruptible, by the word of God, which liveth and abideth for ever" (1 Pet. 1:23). The Blessed Man knows that "whatsoever a man soweth, that shall he also reap. For he that soweth to his flesh shall of the flesh reap corruption; but he that soweth to the Spirit shall of the Spirit reap life everlasting" (Gal. 6:7, 8). Shelley wrote:

> The One remains, the many change and pass;
> Heaven's light forever shines, Earth's shadows fly;
> Life, like a dome of many-colored glass,
> Stains the white radiance of Eternity,
> Until Death tramples it to fragments.

The psalmist goes on to say that "whatsoever he doeth shall prosper." What tremendous promises are in the Word of God! Promises that are as sure as He Who made them. Promises that will be fulfilled if it means moving Heaven and Hell, earth and sea, men and demons! The omnipotence of God stands back of these promises. The wisdom of God guarantees these promises. The love of God motivates these promises. God challenges our hearts with these promises. God dares us to "seek first the kingdom of God and His righteousness" if we want to see His power provide for all our needs. God declares, "Call unto me, and I will answer thee, and shew thee great and mighty things, which thou knowest not" (Jer. 33:3). We are assured that God is "able to do exceeding abundantly above all that we ask or think" (Eph. 3:20). How God desires to lift us above our circumstances, above our temptations, above the mundane cares of the flesh, above the nominal Christendom of our day. He would have us "sit together in heavenly places in Christ Jesus" (Eph. 2:6).

What a large and awesome promise! "Whatsoever he doeth shall prosper." This promise, remember, is not given promiscuously. This promise is given to the man who "delights in the law of the LORD." Psalm 37:4 bears on this: "Delight thyself also in the LORD; and he shall give thee the desires of thine heart." The Lord Jesus Christ said, "If ye abide in me, and my words abide in you, ye shall ask what ye will, and it shall be done unto you" (John 15:7). God's resources are given to those who want God more than anything else in all of the universe. To a man whose heart is satisfied to do the will of God, the promise is — "whatsoever he doeth shall prosper."

Are you a Christian businessman? Is God first in your business? Then claim the promise! "Cast thy bread upon the waters: for thou shalt find it after many days" (Eccles. 11:1). Are you a schoolteacher? Then teach with every expectation that God will prosper that work which you are doing for His glory. Are you a parent? Then "Train up a child in the way he should go: and when he is old, he will not depart from it" (Prov. 22:6). Are you a preacher of the Word of God? Then believe that God's Word is never given in vain, for God promises: "So shall my word be that goeth forth out of my mouth: it shall not return unto me void, but it shall accomplish that which I please, and it shall prosper in the thing whereto I sent it" (Isa. 55:11).

The gardens of earth may turn into deserts and the flowers of earth may fade, but the one who lives for Christ will prosper throughout eternal ages. Man's scientific achievements will someday be burned in a catastrophic conflagration that will engulf the world, but "they that turn many to righteousness [shall shine] as the stars for ever and ever" (Dan. 12:3). The sinful pleasures of men will end in the painful perdition of Hell, but "the sufferings of this present time are not worthy to be compared with the glory which shall be revealed in us" (Rom. 8:18).

Sometime, somewhere in eternity you may see the glorious results of that gospel tract you gave to someone who seemed to be uninterested. Someone may walk up to you on the streets of gold in that eternal city and tell you that your intercession on their behalf was not in vain. So, "let us not be weary in well doing: for in due season we shall reap, if we faint not" (Gal. 6:9).

The world may scoff at the gospel you preach. Satanic wiles may dog your footsteps all the way through life. Hell may rage and death may threaten to undo you. You may wonder if your work can endure the ravages of time and the assaults of the grave, but do not forget that the Lord Jesus Christ has promised the Body of Christ that "the gates of hell shall not prevail against it" (Matt. 16:18). Herod chopped off the head of John the Baptist, but he could not stop the work which John had put into motion. The Jews stoned Stephen's body into a helpless and lifeless hulk, but they did not nor could they ever stop the message which Stephen proclaimed. Nero chopped off Paul's head, but Paul's work lives on while Nero is a black mark on the pages of history. "Therefore, my beloved brethren, be ye stedfast, unmoveable, always abounding in the work of the Lord, forasmuch as ye know that your labour is not in vain in the Lord" (1 Cor. 15:58).

BANEFUL STUBBLE

I. The Distinctiveness of the Contrast

    A. The ungodly man is planted poorly.

    B. The ungodly man is producing painfully.

    C. The ungodly man is poverty-stricken perpetually.

II. The Descriptiveness of the Chaff

    A. Worthless

    B. Useless

III. The Decisiveness of the Condemnation

    A. The fairness of it

    B. The firmness of it

    C. The finality of it

CHAPTER FOUR

Baneful Stubble

*"The ungodly are not so: but are like the chaff
which the wind driveth away" (Ps. 1:4).*

GOOD PHOTOGRAPHERS know the importance of *contrast* in the making of a picture of quality and excellence. If the black and white and gray values are not properly balanced and contrasted, the picture is flat. The photographer must be careful to bring the highlight and shadow areas of his scene into a relationship that will communicate to the person later looking at the picture a true idea of that scene. A good photographer can control the contrast of a picture by increased or decreased shutter speeds, by varying the methods of film development or by using different types of film. Being able to portray accurately the shadow areas of a scene is many times as important to the work of a photographer as properly emphasizing the highlight area of the scene or subject.

The psalmist is a master in the art of contrast. His ability to make "word photographs" is matchless. In fact, it is God-inspired. To be sure, the entire Bible masterfully pictures the glories of God by contrasting them against the dark and ominous background of sin and Satanic-inspired rebellion. The psalmist has described for us in the first three verses of Psalm 1 the characteristics of the Blessed Man.

These characteristics are made even more brilliant when the psalmist compares this Blessed Man to the ungodly.

How replete with contrasts is the Bible's message concerning God's dealings with men! God's grace is set against man's greed. The love of God is in infinite contrast to the lust of the flesh. The mercy of God stands out in bold relief to the meanness of men. The wisdom of God is in contrast to the foolishness of men. Sin is likened to darkness and righteousness is synonymous with light. The Bible tells us that sinful men are "like the troubled sea, when it cannot rest" (Isa. 57:20), while the believer is said to have "peace that passeth all understanding."

This contrast between God and man is so great that Paul writes: "The foolishness of God is wiser than men; and the weakness of God is stronger than men" (1 Cor. 1:25). God says, "For my thoughts are not your thoughts, neither are your ways my ways. . . . For as the heavens are higher than the earth, so are my ways higher than your ways, and my thoughts than your thoughts" (Isa. 55:8, 9). This contrast is evident when we look around us to see what men feel is the important message in life. How would men change this sin-infested world? How would men go about bringing sin-cursed individuals into a life of joy and peace? The Bible says that the gospel is "the power of God." We are commanded to preach the gospel. God says that the simple message of the gospel of Christ is what men need more than anything else.

Scores upon scores of professing preachers do not believe this. They have been taken in by the wisdom of the world. To them, the gospel is too simple to solve all problems. They prefer sociology to salvation. They believe the answer is in economics, not evangelism. They prefer to be tactful diplomats in the world instead of ambassadors for Christ to the world. They feel that reformation is just as effective as regeneration. Their confidence in culture far exceeds their confidence in Christ. Their preaching dwells upon the wonders of progress instead of the blessedness of pardon. They do not mind discussing the new social order, but they ignore the new birth. They will serve on the committee of a new organization, but they are not interested in the truth that if any man be in Christ, he is a new creation.

Yes, there is contrast in this universe.

> God hath chosen the foolish things of the world to confound the wise; and God hath chosen the weak things of the world to confound the things which are mighty;
>
> And base things of the world, and things which are despised, hath God chosen, yea, and things which are not, to bring to nought things that are:
>
> That no flesh should glory in his presence (1 Cor. 1:27-29).

God desires to make known His greatness and glory. He is the Exalted One. All of man's ingenuity, ability and prowess can never accomplish what God can do through lives that are yielded to Him. God takes foolish, weak, base, unrecognized men and redeems them. Then He fills these vessels with His power and shows the self-righteous world that His grace can do more than all of their religions put together.

Moses had a rod, David a slingshot, Gideon a pitcher, Shamgar an oxgoad — all of these things were insignificant items in the hands of unheralded men. But God used these things and these men to defeat armies and individuals whose praises had been sung by the worldly men of those days. God will be glorified among the heathen. "Every tongue should confess that Jesus Christ is Lord, to the glory of God the Father" (Phil. 2:11). You are going to glorify God willingly or unwillingly, but you will glorify Him. In the picture that is this universe, God is the center of attention. All of the battles, all of the experiences, all of the writings, all of the accomplishments of men are just component parts of the contrasting background that serves to exalt more brilliantly the magnificence of our Lord. How glorious is the resurrection of Christ when contrasted with the rugged, dark, cruel, ignominious crucifixion of Christ three days earlier! How wondrous does the grace of God

appear to men when God transforms a sin-bound individual into a Spirit-controlled believer! What a difference
there is between the believer and the unbeliever!

This is the tremendous contrast which the psalmist
brings out so vividly in this First Psalm, a contrast between
the blessed and the baneful.

I. The Distinctiveness of the Contrast

Note carefully the words "the ungodly are not so."
ARE NOT SO! All that has been said about the Blessed Man
is not true of the ungodly man. There is a difference between the believer and the unbeliever. This fact needs to be
emphasized in an age which likes to talk piously about the
Fatherhood of God and the brotherhood of man.

Modern religionists and religious sociologists have
convinced themselves that God is the Father of all men and
that all men are brothers. But is this true? A study of God's
Word will show very definitely that it is not true. God is not
the Father of all men. Neither are all men brothers.

The Bible teaches that God created Adam and Eve in
His own image. But Adam and Eve deliberately sinned
against God. They, so to speak, walked out on God. They
fell from their state of innocence. Their perfect fellowship
with God was broken. God had to drive them out of the
Garden of Eden.

Eve then gave birth to children. Cain and Abel were
born. Later, other children were born to Adam and Eve. All
of these children were born sinners. They were not children of God. They were children of sinful Adam and Eve.
They, like all other children born since, "were by nature
the children of wrath." The apostle Paul also calls all of the
descendants of Adam and Eve "the children of disobedience" (Eph. 2:2). Men are *not* the children of God when
they are born into this world. They are the children of a
sinful father and mother.

The Bible reveals that there are two families in this
world. The one family is made up of those who have been
born just once. They are the children of the Devil. All men

are members of this family until they are born again. The other family is made up of all those who have accepted Christ as Savior and have been born again. This is the family of God.

The worldly religionists like to say that all men are brothers and that all men are sons of God their Father. But this is *not* taught in the Scriptures. Are all men born or created equal? Intellectually, no. Socially, no. Financially, no. Politically, no. Physically, no. Spiritually, yes. All men are born "dead in trespasses and sins" (Eph. 2:1). Each of us could well and truly testify with David: "Behold, I was shapen in iniquity; and in sin did my mother conceive me" (Ps. 51:5).

The Lord Jesus Christ revealed that all men outside of Him are brothers, but their father is the Devil. Adam and Eve had chosen to listen to the Devil instead of God, and this has been true of all their descendants. Thus, men are naturally members of the Devil's family. The world would be more accurate to talk of the "fatherhood of the Devil." Man naturally may be brilliant intellectually. He may be well-adjusted socially. He may have amassed many material possessions. He may have high moral standards. But this does not change the fact that he is a child of the Devil. You slander the Devil when you do not consider him to be intellectually brilliant, socially acceptable, materially wealthy and morally acceptable. The Devil does not want people to become drunkards. The Devil wanted Adam and Eve to become like gods. The Devil wants men to be their best, but without God. The Devil's masterpiece is not a drunken, bleary-eyed bum in the gutter— that is the Devil's failure. The Devil's masterpiece is a self-righteous, morally good, well-thought-of citizen who, for all practical purposes, is an example of a good man, but on his own without God.

The Pharisees were satanic masterpieces. These Pharisees were religious. They were morally upright. They were respected citizens. They were community leaders. They were everything and more than the average unsaved, unconverted church member is today. They thought of themselves as God's children. They thought of themselves as acceptable to God. But listen to what the Lord Jesus Christ said to them in John 8:42-44: "If God were your Father, ye would love me: for I proceeded forth and came from God; neither came I of myself, but he sent me. Why do ye not understand my speech? even because ye cannot hear my word. Ye are of your father the devil, and the lusts of your father ye will do." These Pharisees were children of the Devil just like everyone else born into this world.

"If God were your Father, ye would love me," said Christ. Men prove that they are children of the Devil when they refuse to bow the knee to Christ and accept Him as their only hope and their only Savior. When men love their good works and church membership more than they love Christ, they prove that they are not related to God in any way. The Lord told Nicodemus, a ruler of the Jews, "Except a man be born again, he cannot see the kingdom of God" (John 3:3).

That is how you get to be a child of God— you must be born into His family. God is the Father of all who have been *born again*. All men who have been born again are brothers. How are you born again? John 1:12 and 13 says:

> But as many as received him [Christ], to them gave he power to become the sons of God, even to them that believe on his name:
> Which were born, not of blood, nor of the will of the flesh, nor of the will of man, but of God.

Adam and Eve were children of God because they were created directly by God. You become a child of God only as you are born directly of God. That is why the apostle Paul wrote 2 Corinthians 5:17: "Therefore if any man be in Christ, he is a new creature." He has been born of God! With this great truth rejoicing his heart, Charles Wesley wrote these words:

> Forever here my rest shall be,
> Close to Thy bleeding side.
> This all my hope, and all my plea,
> "For me the Saviour died."

My dying Saviour, and my God,
Fountain for guilt and sin,
Sprinkle me ever with Thy blood,
And cleanse, and keep me clean.

Wash me, and make me thus Thine own;
Wash me, and mine Thou art;
Wash me, but not my feet alone—
My hands, my head, my heart.

The atonement of Thy blood apply,
Till faith to sight improve;
Till hope in full fruition die,
And all my soul be love.

Yes, there is a *distinctive contrast* between the Blessed Man and the ungodly man. There is an infinite difference between the Christ-rejecting sinner and the Christ-accepting believer, a difference as distinct as the difference between Heaven and Hell, life and death, peace and torment, light and darkness, God and Satan. Note the difference as presented by the psalmist.

The Blessed Man	*The Ungodly Man*
Planted Properly	Planted Poorly
Producing Perennially	Producing Painfully
Prospering Prolifically	Poverty-stricken Perpetually

Now let us comment on this comparison. Of course, other comparisons could also be made. For instance, the Blessed Man does not walk in the counsel of the ungodly, nor stand in the way of sinners, nor sit in the seat of the scornful. The ungodly man is on the broad road to destruction, and he has many companions on that road. Proverbs 13:20 tells us that "a companion of fools shall be destroyed."

The Blessed Man delights in the law of the Lord. The believer is a Bible student and he gets great joy out of Bible study. The ungodly man does not delight in the Word of God. He may study it critically or scientifically or curiously, but to him the Bible seems as "foolishness," wrote

Paul in 1 Corinthians 2:14. I have had many unsaved people say to me, "I just don't get anything out of the Bible when I do read it. I can't understand it." Satan's most fierce attacks have always been on the veracity of the Bible. He hates the Bible. He seeks to undermine its authority. That is why modernists and infidels of all ages have endeavored to destroy the doctrine of the verbal inspiration of the Bible.

The Blessed Man meditates day and night in the Word of God. He seeks to bring every thought into captivity to Christ. The ungodly man's mind can be summed up in the words of Genesis 6:5: "Every imagination of the thoughts of his heart was only evil continually." Once when I was in the barbershop getting my hair cut, a man came in, cursing and swearing. He was using the name of Jesus Christ and God and Hell in a disgusting manner. I spoke reprimandingly to him. Do you know what his reply was? He said, "I'm sorry; I guess it's just a habit." But that is not the answer. A man swears because he has a profane heart and mind. "Out of the abundance of the heart the mouth speaketh." The Bible declares that the carnal mind is enmity against God, and until a man is born again he cannot bring "into captivity every thought to the obedience of Christ" (2 Cor. 10:5).

But our main concern in comparing these two types of individuals is their likeness to trees. The Lord Jesus Christ said, "Even so every good tree bringeth forth good fruit; but a corrupt tree bringeth forth evil fruit. A good tree cannot bring forth evil fruit, neither can a corrupt tree bring forth good fruit" (Matt. 7:17, 18). The contrast of which the Lord speaks is that which the psalmist stresses with the words "THE UNGODLY ARE NOT SO."

First, the ungodly are not like the blessed in the matter of *planting*. The Blessed Man is planted properly. But the ungodly man is *planted poorly*. He is planted in the sands of his own self-righteousness and religion and knowledge. Christ likens the ungodly man to "a foolish man, which built his house upon the sand: And the rain descended, and the floods came, and the winds blew, and beat upon that house; and it fell: and great was the fall of it" (Matt. 7:26,

27). The ungodly man cannot say with the Blessed Man, "He brought me up also out of an horrible pit, out of the miry clay, and set my feet upon a rock, and established my goings" (Ps. 40:2). The ungodly man does not have the testimony of songwriter Edward Mote, who wrote:

> My hope is built on nothing less
> Than Jesus' blood and righteousness;
> I dare not trust the sweetest frame,
> But wholly lean on Jesus' name.
>
> When darkness veils His lovely face,
> I rest on His unchanging grace;
> In ev'ry high and stormy gale
> My anchor holds within the veil.
>
> His oath, His covenant, His blood,
> Support me in the whelming flood;
> When all around my soul gives way,
> He then is all my hope and stay.
>
> When He shall come with trumpet sound,
> O may I then in Him be found,
> Dressed in His righteousness alone,
> Faultless to stand before the throne.
>
> On Christ, the solid Rock, I stand—
> All other ground is sinking sand,
> All other ground is sinking sand.

Second, the ungodly are not like the blessed in the matter of *production* or *fruitfulness*. The Blessed Man is producing good fruit perennially. He "comes with rejoicing bringing his sheaves with him." But the ungodly are not so! The ungodly *produce painfully*. Paul wrote: "He that soweth to his flesh shall of the flesh reap corruption" (Gal. 6:8). James explained the painful results of man's sowing to the flesh when he said: "But every man is tempted, when he is drawn away of his own lust, and enticed. Then when lust hath conceived, it bringeth forth sin: and sin, when it is finished, bringeth forth death" (James 1:14, 15). Eliphaz sounded this solemn note: "Even as I have seen, they that plow iniquity, and sow wickedness, reap the same. By the blast of God they perish, and by the breath of his nostrils are they consumed" (Job 4:8, 9).

Third, the ungodly differ from the blessed in the matter of prosperity. While the Blessed Man is prospering prolifically, the ungodly man is *poverty-stricken perpetually.* Now we are not speaking of material and financial prosperity, for the unbeliever is oftentimes well-to-do as far as material blessings are concerned. But "what shall it profit a man, if he shall gain the whole world, and lose his own soul?" (Mark 8:36). The ungodly man is one whose whole life is spent for that which is temporal and fleeting. Throughout eternity he is a pauper. The ungodly man is epitomized in Luke 16 where the Lord Jesus Christ tells of "a certain rich man, which was clothed in purple and fine linen, and fared sumptuously every day." That sounds pretty good, doesn't it? But go on. "The rich man also died, and was buried; And in hell he lift up his eyes, being in torments." Do not ever forget it! "It is appointed unto men once to die!" (Heb. 9:27). This rich man had made all kinds of elaborate preparation for life, but he made *no* preparation for death and eternity. He was prosperous in time but poverty-stricken eternally. How much better to be poor in the things of time and rich in the valuables of eternity!

What is the element that makes this distinctive difference? That element is a Person, and that Person is Jesus Christ. John put it succinctly and unmistakably: "He that hath the Son hath life; and he that hath not the Son of God hath not life" (1 John 5:12). If you have Christ as your Savior, you are eternally rich. If you do not have Christ, regardless of whatever else you may possess, you are a pauper. Ponder the inspired words of the apostle Paul: "For ye know the grace of our Lord Jesus Christ, that, though he was rich, yet for your sakes he became poor, that ye through his poverty might be rich" (2 Cor. 8:9).

Perhaps you ask, Who is ungodly? An ungodly person is a person without God and God's righteousness. How can you have God and God's righteousness? ONLY IN CHRIST! Jesus said, "No man cometh unto the Father, but by me." The apostle Paul tells us that in Christ "dwelleth all the fulness of the Godhead bodily" (Col. 2:9). Again, Paul instructs us that "the righteousness of God . . . is by faith of Jesus Christ unto all and upon all them that believe" (Rom. 3:22). Note carefully the words *unto* and *upon*. Paul is saying that the righteousness of God is not something you earn or pay for. It is an absolute gift purchased at Calvary by the Lord Jesus Christ's blood. Paul assures us that it is "not by works of righteousness which we have done, but according to his mercy he saved us" (Titus 3:5). You see, we are talking about GOD'S righteousness, not YOURS. The Bible says that "all our righteousnesses are as filthy rags" (Isa. 64:6).

The Pharisees had plenty of their own righteousness, but they were still ungodly. People today like to talk about their good works and their good intentions, but all of that is man's righteousness, not God's. In order to have eternal life and forgiveness of sin, you need God's righteousness, and this is only available from God as a gift. "The gift of God is eternal life through Jesus Christ our Lord" (Rom. 6:23). Now, go back to Romans 3:22 where Paul says that this righteousness of God is by faith unto and upon all them that what?— "that believe." That is what God wants you to do. He wants you to accept His gift. "Believe on the Lord Jesus Christ, and thou shalt be saved" (Acts 16:31). "He that hath the Son hath life." Is it that simple? Yes, it is that simple. For when you have Christ, you have the treasure of Heaven, and all of God's wondrous resources are at your disposal. Christ is the difference between light and darkness, peace and torment, life and death, Heaven and Hell— Christ is the difference. He can transform your life if you will invite Him into your heart and life.

II. The Descriptiveness of the Chaff

The psalmist describes the ungodly by saying they are "like the chaff." Chaff is the refuse or husks of the grain. It is separated from the seed by threshing. After the threshing has been completed, the grain is thrown into the air, and the light chaff and straw are blown away.

Chaff is worthless and useless. This is certainly descriptive of the ungodly man, for he is and has nothing that is worthy before God. Until the ungodly man is willing to admit his unworthiness and sinfulness, there is little hope for him. The apostle Paul wrote, "For I know that in me (that is, in my flesh,) dwelleth no good thing" (Rom. 7:18). Isaiah confessed: "But we are all as an unclean thing, and all our righteousnesses are as filthy rags; and we all do fade as a leaf; and our iniquities, like the wind, have taken us away" (Isa. 64:6). The wise author of the Proverbs admits that even the "plowing of the wicked, is sin" (Prov. 21:4).

The unworthiness of the ungodly man and the uselessness of his works of self-righteousness will be clearly evident at the judgment. The Lord Jesus Christ describes this solemn occasion in Matthew 7:21-23:

> Not every one that saith unto me, Lord, Lord, shall enter into the kingdom of heaven; but he that doeth the will of my Father which is in heaven.
> Many will say to me in that day, Lord, Lord, have we not prophesied in thy name? and in thy name have we cast out devils? and in thy name done many wonderful works?
> And then will I profess unto them, I never knew you: depart from me, ye that work iniquity.

There it is — prophesying, casting out devils, many wonderful works — ALL of them worthless and useless chaff! Human effort simply does not avail before God.

Eternal value is found only in the work of Christ. When He saves us and indwells us and lives through us, then, and only then, are our lives of eternal value to God.

III. The Decisiveness of the Condemnation

Early on the morning of August 6, 1945, a B-29 plane named the *Enola Gay* took off from an American base located in the Pacific. The *Enola Gay* was piloted by Colonel Paul W. Tibbetts, Jr., of Miami, Florida. At 8:15 A.M. Colonel Tibbetts was over the city of Hiroshima, Japan. The order, "Bombs away," was given. The first atomic bomb plummeted toward the city, and a sudden, sickening, roaring, blinding, agnozing explosion blasted 80,000 souls into eternity! Without warning, without any time to get ready, those thousands of lives were snuffed out!

After that blast had taken place, there was no calling it back. It was terrifyingly decisive! That explosion destroyed from 62,000 to 90,000 buildings. No wonder! That atomic bomb had explosive power the equivalent of 20,000 tons of TNT. That bomb was intended to be conclusive, and for 80,000 lives, it was indeed conclusive.

But what happened on August 6, 1945, is not nearly as awesome in its consequences as what will happen someday to every one of the millions of people who brazenly reject the Son of God. Our Lord said, "Fear not them which kill the body, but are not able to kill the soul: but rather fear him which is able to destroy both soul and body in hell" (Matt. 10:28). Those people in Hiroshima lost their physical lives, but someday those bodies will be joined again to their souls in order to stand judgment. Those souls right now are either in Heaven or Hell, depending upon whether or not they belonged to Jesus Christ. And when God decides that "time shall be no more," then will come the awesome events which will culminate in the eternal torment of both the bodies and souls of unbelievers.

The ungodly are "like the chaff which the wind driveth away," wrote the psalmist. Note that decisive "driveth away!" John the Baptist spoke of the Lord Jesus Christ when he said,

> He shall baptize you with the Holy Ghost and with fire:
> Whose fan is in his hand, and he will throughly purge his floor, and will gather the wheat into his garner; but the chaff he will burn with fire unquenchable (Luke 3:16, 17).

Christ is the almighty thresher and winnower Whose condemnation of the ungodly will be final. There will be no
possibility of appeals, for He is the Supreme Judge of all the
earth.

We need more emphasis on the finality of God's
judgments. We live in a morally lax generation when men
glibly and blasphemously talk of God as the Man Upstairs.
Men wink at the solemn declarations of the Bible concerning coming condemnation. God is looked upon as some
senile old Grandfather Whose word can be taken with a
grain of salt. When Hell is mentioned, twentieth-century,
sophisticated "intellects" laughingly explain that Hell will
probably be air-conditioned. What must an almighty, holy,
omnipotent God think of this sinful and adulterous generation?

We need to be reminded that "he that believeth not is
condemned already, because he hath not believed in the
name of the only begotten Son of God" (John 3:18). This
means, dear reader, that if you are right now a Christ-
rejector, you are under the condemnation of God. "The
wrath of God abides" on you. The only way to move out
from under that wrath is to accept the Lord Jesus Christ as
your personal Savior and Substitute. If you refuse to do this
and you die in your sinful, unbelieving condition, you are
irrevocably lost and condemned. Your condemnation will
be far more — an eternity more — devastating than was
the physical condemnation of 80,000 Japanese at
Hiroshima.

Think for a moment on the decisiveness of condemnation. When God's judgments fall, they fall certainly and
inexorably, for "God is not a man, that he should lie;
neither the son of man, that he should repent: hath he said,
and shall he not do it? or hath he spoken, and shall he not
make it good?" (Num. 23:19). Think of the judgment of the
Flood. Through His servant Noah, God warned the people
of that generation of the impending judgment. For over a
hundred years the people were exhorted to repent by
Noah, "a preacher of righteousness." They ignored his
pleas. They scoffed at his message. They mocked at the

idea of a worldwide flood. They rejected the doctrine of a holy God who judges sin and unrepenting sinners. Then one day it began to rain. Noah was safely shut up inside the ark. But "the fountains of the great deep [were] broken up, and the windows of heaven were opened" (Gen. 7:11). Judgment had come, and it was so decisive that we read "all that was in the dry land, died" (Gen. 7:22).

A sex-crazy, morally rotten, sensually degraded, perverted generation of people in Sodom and Gomorrah were swaggeringly proud that they were "lovers of pleasure more than lovers of God." Sodom and Gomorrah were so prevailingly debauched that even Abraham knew he would be unable to find ten righteous people there. Those inhabitants of Sodom and Gomorrah were the predecessors of the Hollywood movie crowd. They were "too wise" and "progressive" to believe that God really meant it when He said, "Thou shalt not commit adultery." After all, marriages were just convenient makeshifts until another lover came along! So reasoned those wicked people. They made fun of morality and decency and modesty. When Lot finally opened his mouth to cry out against this cesspool of iniquity, "he seemed as one that mocked unto his sons in law" (Gen. 19:14). Then judgment fell! "Then the LORD rained upon Sodom and upon Gomorrah brimstone and fire from the LORD out of heaven" (Gen. 19:24). Yes, the "ungodly are like the chaff which the wind driveth away."

The Blessed Man looks forward to meeting God, for "there is . . . no condemnation to them which are in Christ Jesus" (Rom. 8:1). But the ungodly man, whether he claims to be atheistic, agnostic or materialistic, has no real desire to give any serious thought to the hereafter. For the ungodly man, eternity is a dark mystery that is best not talked about and even less meditated upon. The people of Noah's day did not believe in judgment, either, but it came. The cynical and pleasure-mad throngs of Sodom and Gomorrah did not believe that fundamentalist "nonsense" about the hell fire and damnation, either, but the fire and brimstone came anyway.

And all of the incessant endeavors of men to explain

away or reason away or philosophize away the eternal truths of the Bible with relationship to Heaven and Hell are just evidences that deep down in the souls of these men is the innate knowledge that these truths are so. Thus, ungodly man, in his endeavor to still the voice of that gnawing sense of final judgment, writes and reasons and educates himself into believing otherwise. But all to no avail!

In the second chapter of Daniel, God reveals to Daniel the interpretation of Nebuchadnezzar's dream. Daniel reveals that the image which Nebuchadnezzar saw represents the Gentile powers which will rule in the world until the "times of the Gentiles" have come to an end. God reveals that all of the accomplishments that ungodly men may be able to achieve will come to nought when the Lord Jesus Christ returns. "Then was the iron, the clay, the brass, the silver, and the gold, broken to pieces together, and become like the chaff of the summer threshingfloors; and the wind carried them away, that no place was found for them: and the stone that smote the image became a great mountain, and filled the whole earth" (Dan. 2:35). What Daniel here reveals concerning the powers of the Gentiles is true of all that ungodly men will ever be or do.

Without Christ the human mind's an ugly grave
Where, enthroned, a sin-cursed will all thoughts deprave.
Where men scheme and plot in hopeful melancholy
Their worldly ways, their hellish plans and godless folly.

Without Christ the human heart's an empty thing
From whence the soul its sins and woes cannot fling.
Its hopes, its joys, it songs all seem as foolish bubbles
When thought of death or judgment its conscience ill troubles.

Without Christ the human life's a vain charade
Where men toil, spend and sweat their works to parade.
Works that beneath God's eye and time's dusty rubble
Will all be judged and burned as baneful stubble.

BANEFUL SHAME

I. The Inability of the Ungodly

   A. No place to hide

   B. No plea to herald

   C. No power to help

II. An Illustration of the Ungodly (Judas Iscariot)

   A. The deceiver of the disciples

   B. The dupe of the Devil

      1. Filthy lucre lured Judas.

      2. The father of lies led Judas.

   C. The deliverer of Deity

      1. The student failed his Teacher.

      2. The disciple defected from his Lord.

      3. The subject betrayed the King.

      4. The sinner sold the Savior.

CHAPTER FIVE

Baneful Shame

"Therefore the ungodly shall not stand in the judgment, nor sinners in the congregation of the righteous" (Ps. 1:5).

UNGODLY! It is an ugly looking word, is it not? Ungodly men are heading for a meeting with God! The Bible tells us that Christ has a score to settle with the ungodly.

> ... Behold, the Lord cometh with ten thousands of his saints,
> To execute judgment upon all, and to convince all that are *ungodly* among them of all their *ungodly* deeds which they have *ungodly* committed, and of all their hard speeches which *ungodly* sinners have spoken against him (Jude 14, 15).

When the Lord Jesus Christ returns the second time, top priority will be given to the judgment of the ungodly.

In this chapter we want to identify the ungodly both as to his person and his plight. He is an outcast from God and from God's people.

I. The Inability of the Ungodly

The ungodly man "shall not stand in the judgment, nor sinners in the congregation of the righteous." The sinner's inability is vividly portrayed for us by the apostle John in Revelation 20:11-15. In these verses is given to us a description of the Great White Throne Judgment at which all sinners must appear. Note carefully John's words.

> And I saw a great white throne, and him that sat on it, from whose face the earth and the heaven fled away; and there was found no place for them.
> And I saw the dead, small and great, stand before God; and the books were opened: and another book was opened, which is the book of life: and the dead were judged out of those things which were written in the books, according to their works.
> And the sea gave up the dead which were in it; and death and hell delivered up the dead which were in them: and they were judged every man according to their works.
> And death and hell were cast into the lake of fire. This is the second death.
> And whosoever was not found written in the book of life was cast into the lake of fire.

In the verses we have quoted from Revelation, we find the terrible plight of the ungodly man to be along three distinct lines of moral inability.

First, he will, at the judgment, have *no place to hide*. The all-seeing, ever-searching eye of God at last will have brought the sinner to the place of accounting. No more delays, no more excuses, no more postponements. THE JUDGMENT HAS COME. The facades of pride, the varnished veneer of culture, the whitewash of education, the makeup of self-righteousness — all of these masks have been torn away, and the ungodly faces God with guilt written on his every expression, sin impressed on his every feature, ungodliness testified to in his every word.

If the sinner could express his plight in poetry, he might say with the writer of Psalm 139:7-12:

> Whither shall I go from thy spirit? or whither shall
> I flee from thy presence?
> If I ascend up into heaven, thou art there: if I

make my bed in hell, behold, thou art there.

If I take the wings of the morning, and dwell in the uttermost parts of the sea;

Even there shall thy hand lead me, and thy right hand shall hold me.

If I say, Surely the darkness shall cover me; even the night shall be light about me.

Yea, the darkness hideth not from thee; but the night shineth as the day: the darkness and the light are both alike to thee.

NO PLACE TO HIDE! Christ-rejecting sinner reading these words right now, you cannot forever hide from God. You can evade the preacher; you can ignore the Sunday school teacher; you can stay away from the church; you can refuse to open your Bible; BUT, you must, you will meet God at the judgment. *This is certain.*

Second, the sinner will, at the judgment, have *no plea to herald.* The psalmist tells us that the ungodly man will not be able to stand in the judgment. In other words, he will have no defense. His reasons will not be valid; his excuses will not be acceptable; his answers will not be plausible. *He will be defenseless.* The apostle Paul informs us that God has so convincingly convicted men of their guilt in His Law so that "every mouth may be stopped, and all the world may become guilty before God" (Rom. 3:19). Since this is so, the time to admit one's guilt and plead for mercy is NOW, while you may still accept the Christ Who alone can free you from your guilt. To wait until the judgment day is to be too late!

The ungodly man will have no defense because he does not have the Lord Jesus Christ. He is the only defense. Only if you have been written in the Lamb's Book of Life by giving your heart and life to God through the acceptance of His Son can you escape the consequences of sin. John wrote, "Whosoever was not found written in the book of life was cast into the lake of fire" (Rev. 20:15).

Third, the sinner will, at the judgment, have *no power to help.* Some Christ-rejectors have great confidence in "keeping the Law." But the Bible warns us that there is no power in endeavoring to keep the Law. Paul so instructs us in Romans 3:20: "By the deeds of the law there shall no flesh be justified in his sight: for by the law is the knowledge of sin." So, having tried to keep the Ten Commandments will mean absolutely nothing at the judgment. Only one Person has fully kept the Ten Commandments, and that One is Jesus Christ. That is why God wants you to accept Christ — because Christ's righteousness will be accepted on your behalf. But God will have nothing to do with sinful men who prefer their *attempts* at righteousness to Christ's *accomplishment* of righteousness.

Still others put a great deal of confidence in the power of money. But be sure that God is one Judge Who will never be bribed or in the least influenced by the riches of any man. Peter reminds us that our salvation comes through the blood of Christ, not through the payment of our money. He writes:

> Ye know that ye were not redeemed with corruptible things, as silver and gold, from your vain conversation received by tradition from your fathers;
> But with the precious blood of Christ, as of a lamb without blemish and without spot (1 Pet. 1:18, 19).

Other sinners somehow think that their religion will give them special powers at the judgment. This, too, is fallacy. The apostle Paul, who, before he was converted, was a very religious Pharisee, has this to say about the efficacy of religious works:

> Not by works of righteousness which we have done, but according to his mercy he saved us, by the washing of regeneration, and renewing of the Holy Ghost;
> Which he shed on us abundantly through Jesus Christ our Saviour;
> That being justified by his grace, we should be made heirs according to the hope of eternal life (Titus 3:5-7).

To have Christ is to have God. To have God is to escape eternal judgment. Since the Christ-rejecting sinner does not have Christ, he does not have God; thus he stands at the judgment hopelessly, helplessly, horrendously condemned. Only the Lord Jesus can save men from sin and the consequences of that sin.

II. An Illustration of the Ungodly

On June 14, 1801, a disgraced, poverty-stricken man died in London, England. His name was Benedict Arnold. This man's name has become synonymous with the term *treason,* for it was Benedict Arnold who went over to the side of the British during the Revolutionary War. General George Washington had trusted the military skill of Arnold so much that he had given him the command of West Point, which was strategically important to the control of the entire Hudson Valley. Arnold betrayed the confidence of Washington and the Revolutionary leaders by plotting with Sir Henry Clinton to deliver West Point into the hands of the British. Fortunately, the plot was discovered and the American cause was saved, but the name of Benedict Arnold lives on as a symbol of treason. Arnold sold his country for about 6,300 pounds. This was the price he exacted from General Clinton for informing him of the American plans. Arnold was a ruined and disgraced man after this. To a true American, no one has ever been more un-American than Arnold.

But I want to tell you about a man whose treason is blacker than that of Benedict Arnold. I want to tell you about a man who sold his Lord and his fellow workers to the enemy for a price far less than 6,300 pounds. This man sold his Lord to the enemy for just thirty pieces of silver, the equivalent of less than ten English pounds. The name of this traitor was Judas Iscariot. I believe that Judas Iscariot is the most ungodly man ever portrayed on the pages of Holy Writ. An examination of this man will reveal just what the Bible means when it speaks of the ungodly. The Lord Jesus Christ called Judas Iscariot "the son of perdition." The

Bible tells us that "Satan entered into" Judas (John 13:27). For an illustration of ungodliness, we need not examine Adolph Hitler or Joseph Stalin or Nero. Look at Judas!

When I think of Judas Iscariot, I compare his sin with that of other men whose dark deeds live on the pages of history; but I find no other man who is so notorious as this man. Judas was more contemptible than Ahab; more greedy than Balaam; more cruel than Cain; more proud than Diotrophes; more foolish than Esau; more hardened than Felix; more arrogant than Goliath; more deceitful than Herod; more mocking than Ishmael; more disgusting than Jezebel.

The sin of Judas was a conspiracy more deadly than that of Korah; a betrayal more brazen than that of Laban; a memory more shameful than that of Meroz; a crime more dastardly than that of Naboth; an offense more insulting that that of Oreb; a rebellion more obstinate than that of Pharaoh; an instability more disastrous than that of Reuben; a tragedy more heartrending than that of Samson; a taint more indelible than that of Tyre.

The treacherous deed of Judas is a monument to unbelief; a statue to the vain villainy of a vile man; a reminder of the inevitable wages of sin; a record of the consequence ensured by the callous heart of a man indwelt by Satan, the destructive dictator of the forces of Hell; and a solemn assurance that what a man sows, that shall he also reap.

The face of Judas is a portrait of deceit. The speech of Judas is the voice of hypocrisy. The hands of Judas are the instruments of a greedy heart. The eyes of Judas are the darkened windows of a soiled soul curtained by the depraved drapery of human degeneracy. The body of Judas is the dwelling place of the most fearsome of evil spirits, Satan himself.

Philosophy brands Judas a victim of fate; psychiatry calls him a schizophrenic; political science charges him with treason; literature sees him as a villain; music records him as a discord; art portrays him as a sullen shadow; but Jesus Christ declares with somber finality that Judas is the "son of perdition."

Just what was the crime of Judas Iscariot? THE REJEC-
TION OF THE LORD JESUS CHRIST! Yes, to reject Jesus
Christ is the most ungodly act of all ungodly acts. As one
studies the life of Judas, he is surprised to find that Judas
was a trusted man among the apostles of Christ. Ungodliness can sometimes be hidden for a time from man, but the
Lord knew Judas all the time. Recall the words of 1 Samuel
16:7: "But the LORD said unto Samuel, Look not on his
countenance, or on the height of his stature: because I have
refused him: for the LORD seeth not as man seeth; for man
looketh on the outward appearance, but the LORD looketh
on the heart." Only God knows how many Judases are in
our midst, Judases who pay lip service to Jesus Christ but
who in their hearts actually reject and despise Him. Let us
study this man Judas to see what an ungodly man really is.

First, look at Judas, *the deceiver of the disciples.* How
cunning this man was! For over three years he lived with
the disciples, whom he completely fooled. Peter admitted
that Judas "was numbered with us, and had obtained part
of this ministry" (Acts 1:17). Although the Lord Jesus Christ
knew the real Judas Iscariot, He did not convey this knowledge of Judas to the other disciples. Judas was accepted as
one of the Twelve. When Christ sent out the twelve disciples, as recorded in the tenth chapter of Matthew's Gospel,
Judas was one of the commissioned ones. Judas was sent to
the "lost sheep of the house of Israel," and he exercised
God-granted power to heal the sick, to cleanse lepers, to
do many miraculous works; he preached about the kingdom of Heaven; he told many of the Lord Jesus Christ.
Judas was looked upon as a faithful disciple of our Lord.
Yet, he was not faithful; he was a fraud. For three years
Judas ministered with the other eleven disciples. He
traveled with them, ate with them, slept with them and
completely deceived them. They had no idea he was nurs-
ing in his heart the blackest of all deeds.

In Luke 9:54 we are told that on one occasion our
Lord went into a village of the Samaritans and was not well
received. "And when his disciples James and John saw this,
they said, Lord, wilt thou that we command fire to come

down from heaven, and consume them, even as Elias did?"
What righteous indignation these "Sons of Thunder" could
exhibit! What would have been their reaction if they had
known that one of their own company was later to reject
their Lord in a far more ignoble manner than did these
Samaritans? But these two disciples, as well as the rest,
were completely oblivious to the real heart condition of
Judas.

Another proof that Judas was a trusted man among the
apostles is the fact that he was elected treasurer of the
group. Whenever I am introduced to the treasurer of a
church, I assume that he must be a trustworthy individual,
because people do not wish to trust their money to anyone
whose character or reputation is in any way questionable.
So Judas must have been a man who had convinced the
other disciples of his unswerving loyalty to the Lord. Yet
this man, who was to become the epitome of treason, was
the elected treasurer of this tight-knit group of disciples.
How cunning, how clever, how deceitful some ungodly
men can be! More than one individual in most churches is
probably anything but the pious, spiritual giant he claims to
be before his fellow church members.

I once read a news article about the chief of detectives
in one of our large midwestern cities. This chief was caused
a great deal of embarrassment because a neighbor of his in
the apartment building where he lived was caught operating a "bookie joint" in his room. The man who was accept-
ing bets on horses had an apartment three floors above the
chief's apartment. The gambler had been operating his
"bookie joint" for almost a year. The chief of detectives,
who was busy raiding other places all over the city, was
unaware that illegal gambling was taking place right in the
same building where he lived. The chief was quoted as
saying, "This gambling wouldn't have been going on if I
had known it was there." But the fact remains the chief did
not know what was going on; he had had the wool pulled
over his eyes. He had been deceived.

So it was with the disciples. They were deceived by
Judas. His outward profession had convinced them of

Judas's sincerity. His facade appeared to them to be a true representation of what a believer really would be. But he was a traitor. I think this is a great lesson for us. The sham life of Judas the disciple ought to be a warning to all of us not to place our confidence in men, not in human ingenuity, but in the Lord Himself. The writer of Hebrews exhorts us to be constantly "looking unto Jesus the author and finisher of our faith" (Heb. 12:2). Men will deceive you; men will disappoint you; men will fail to live up to your expectation and to their boasts. But Christ will never fail!

We live in a generation of man-worshipers. Teenagers idolize movie stars. Many adults idolize politicians. Such idolatry has been carried over into the religious realm, and many people have all of their faith in Dr. So-and-So or in Bishop What's-His-Name or in Rev. Fiddle-Dee-Dee or in that denomination or organization; but this is not God's will. God desires that we keep our faith and confidence in His dear Son. What a blow it must have been to the disciples when the real Judas Iscariot was revealed! What a stirring of the soul must have taken place in the heart of the beloved John when Judas was unveiled as a traitor! What a shock it must have been to the hundreds of people who had been encouraged by Judas to follow Jesus. Yes, ungodly Judas was a deceiver of the disciples.

We make this point to emphasize that ungodliness is found in religious circles as well as among the heathen. Judas was religious. He even lived in the company of Christ Himself. He made his vocation that of the ministry of a disciple. Yet in his heart he was as ungodly a man as anyone who ever lived. He knew Christ, but he had not accepted Christ. He heard Christ teach, but Judas never really trusted and fully believed in the Teacher. Judas was all "front" and no "faith." And this is true of many ungodly people today.

Second, look at Judas, *the dupe of the Devil.* The apostle Paul characterizes evil men as "deceiving, and being deceived" (2 Tim. 3:13). This was true of Judas. He was guilty of deceiving the disciples, but he was being deceived by the Devil all the while he was deceiving others. Judas listened to the subtle wooings of Satan. He was taken in by the glowing promises of the Devil. Judas the deceiver who posed as Judas the disciple was easy prey for the master of darkness who poses as an angel of light. Satan shrewdly and deceitfully led Judas down the broad road to utter destruction.

Filthy lucre lured Judas. Satan knew that Judas had a vulnerable spot, an Achilles' heel, a weak place in his character, a flaw in his moral armor. And Satan, as always, knew exactly how best to take advantage of that weakness.

First Timothy 6:9 and 10 tells us:

> But they that will be rich fall into temptation and a snare, and into many foolish and hurtful lusts, which drown men in destruction and perdition.
>
> For the love of money is the root of all evil: which while some coveted after, they have erred from the faith, and pierced themselves through with many sorrows.

Perhaps the apostle Paul thought of Judas as he penned this passage; for Judas craved money, he coveted wealth, he was greedy for gold, he was salacious for silver. Judas, the son of perdition, would be rich, and because of this he literally "drowned in destruction and perdition."

Reader, beware of covetousness! People have been slain; businesses have been wrecked; homes have been broken; love has been dashed upon the rocks; children have been orphaned; wars have been started; countries have gone down the drain of history because of this love for money which is the "root of all evil."

The father of lies led Judas. In John 13:27-30 we read some of the most mysteriously solemn words in the Bible:

> And after the sop Satan entered into him [Judas]. Then said Jesus unto him, That thou doest, do quickly.
>
> Now no man at the table knew for what intent he spake this unto him.
>
> For some of them thought, because Judas had the

bag, that Jesus had said unto him, Buy those things that we have need of against the feast; or, that he should give something to the poor.

He then having received the sop went immediately out: and it was night.

Yes, for Judas it was surely night. It was night physically. It was night intellectually. It was night spiritually. It was night morally. Yea, it was night eternally, for Judas had sold his soul to the powers of darkness. The powers of darkness now directed his every depraved thought, his every perverted step, his every ignominious action. From the time Judas left the Upper Room until he went out and hanged himself, Judas was indwelt and controlled by Satan.

Judas went out into the blackness of betrayal, out into the darkness of damnation, out into eternity without Christ. What a pitiful, painful picture this is! What a message of warning! For the same Satan who so cruelly deceived Judas goes about today to bring men to destruction. Satan is still in the business of ruining the souls of men. The Devil yet delights in turning the hearts of men against the Lord Jesus Christ. Peter, a companion of Judas for three years, penned a message of caution and concern when he wrote: "Be sober, be vigilant; because your adversary the devil, as a roaring lion, walketh about, seeking whom he may devour" (1 Pet. 5:8). Heed the warning of God's Word! Satan is not your friend. He ruined the Garden of Eden, and it is the aim of the Devil to see that Hell is well populated. The Devil delights in nothing more than seeing men neglect, ignore and reject the Lord of Glory, Jesus Christ.

The Devil actually made Judas think that thirty pieces of silver were of more value than the friendship of the Son of God. Satan duped Judas into trading the Truth of God for thirty tarnished coins. Before Judas had the coins long enough to polish them, he found that they were not worth having. He found that the lure of the Devil is a lie, the glitter of sin is a mirage, the promise of the Devil is worthless, and the tinsel of silver is tragedy.

Jesus said, "For what shall it profit a man, if he shall gain the whole world, and lose his own soul? Or what shall a man give in exchange for his soul?" (Mark 8:36, 37). Judas had heard Jesus say that. Yet Judas exchanged his soul— not for the world — but for thirty pieces of silver! O what a fool Satan made of Judas.

Third, look at Judas, *the deliverer of Deity*. Judas was the betrayer of the Bread of Life, traitor to the Truth of God. It was Judas who delivered the Christ into the hands of wicked men to be crucified on Calvary's rugged cross.

Judas the student failed his Teacher. What a Teacher the Lord Jesus Christ was! "No man ever spake as this man!" Jesus was the apex of academic aptness, the excellence of education, the personification of perfect pedagogy. And Judas had the privilege of being one of this Great Teacher's special students.

Judas heard the Beatitudes from Jesus' own lips. He listened as our Lord taught in wonderful simplicity the model prayer. Judas paid close attention as Christ urged men to lay up treasure in Heaven where thieves do not break through and steal. He heard our Savior warn against wolves who come in sheep's clothing. Judas was present when Jesus first gave to His disciples those marvelous parables concerning the sower and the wheat and the tares. He leaned forward so as not to miss a word as the Matchless Master spoke of the hidden treasure and expounded on the pearl of great price.

Judas showed great interest when Jesus gave to the world that instructive and moving story of the Good Samaritan. He must have been deeply impressed as he listened to the compassionate voice of the Savior tell the story of the Prodigal Son for the very first time. Judas must have drawn back just a little when he listened with wonder to the scathing denunciation of the Pharisees by Jesus as recorded in Matthew 23.

Yes, Judas was a student of the world's most expert educator. And yet Judas failed to learn the lessons; he failed to submit himself to what he heard. Instead of a steadily growing affection for his Teacher, Judas nursed a growing rebellion against Him. Judas the student failed Jesus the Teacher.

Someone says, "How terrible! How tragic to sit under the ministry of Jesus Christ and yet remain unsaved!" But think a moment! I know people who sit under the sound of the gospel message week after week, month after month, year after year, and they are not saved yet; they have not yielded to Christ yet. They listen to the preacher talk about the blood of Christ shed in their behalf; they hear that there is a Hell to be saved from and a Heaven to be saved into; they know that life is uncertain and death is inevitable; but still they refuse to renounce their sin and trust Christ. They refuse to act upon what they have heard. The sin of Judas is a common one even today! And the sin of Judas is ungodly. The rejection of Christ is ungodliness at its worst.

Then, notice *Judas the disciple defected from his Lord.* Benedict Arnold was a disgrace to his country because he defected to the enemy just when he was needed and trusted the most. His crime is all the more dastardly because of the trusted position which he held. So the crime of Judas appears all the more repulsive when we see it against the background of his opportunity and privilege as a trusted disciple of the Lord.

One might have expected Jesus to be delivered by the treachery of a Sadducee or by the plottings of the Pharisees or by the machinations of the Herodians. Who would imagine, who would ever dare to think that one of His very own disciples would make the shameful deal and consummate the contemptible conspiracy? But Judas did! He defected to the enemy and delivered his Lord to His enemies.

Also, *Judas the subject betrayed the King of kings.*

> Jesus Christ, King of kings and Lord of lords,
> He Whom angels worship and saints adore,
> Jesus Christ, the Lamb of God for sinners slain,
> Jesus Christ, King of kings and Lord of lords.

Judas Iscariot betrayed this Sovereign One. Out into the night he went. He left divine royalty in the Upper Room to creep through the shadows to the passing potentates of the Sanhedrin in order to sell his King for thirty pieces of silver.

Would you not think that the price of a king would be more? Certainly the betrayal of a sovereign ought to bring a better price than the price of a slave! But Judas is now mastered by Satan. He is hell-bent on his awful deed. What the Devil-inspired leaders of the Sanhedrin offer, Judas takes, and the horrible covenant is sealed.

It was not too many hours after this vile transaction that Jesus Christ hung on Calvary's cross. A sign was placed over His head: "JESUS OF NAZARETH THE KING OF THE JEWS." As Jesus hung there, out on some dark plot of ground was the sinister, swaying shadow of a body. As Jesus hung by nails on the cross, His betrayer hung from a tree by the neck until the tree limb broke and dashed the body of Judas on the rocks below. As Jesus Christ, the Son of God, paid for our sins on the cross, as He cried from the agony of His soul, "My God, my God, why has thou forsaken me?" — even then Judas was crying from the fires of Hell for just one drop of water to cool his parched tongue.

Why did Judas hang himself? Do you recall the words of the psalmist? He said, "The ungodly shall not stand . . . in the congregation of the righteous." Judas had to go out from the disciples because he could no longer stand the company of decent men. Judas had to plunge his soul into Hell by suicide because he could no longer stand the company of righteous men. He could no longer face any of the disciples; he was doomed. Every sinner finally comes to this place, and that is one reason why God had to provide a place called Hell.

But perhaps worse than all other considerations we have meditated upon with reference to Judas is the fact that *Judas the sinner sold the Savior.* Think of it! His only hope for eternal life, his only way of salvation, his only escape from Hell, his only source of real peace, his only true friend was Jesus Christ; YET Judas sold this One.

How many in the world today are doing the very same thing! They are exchanging the Son of God for their thirty pieces of silver. Some sell Him for the silver of meaningless self-righteousness; some barter Him away for church membership; some trade Him for the fleeting plaudits of the masses; but no man ever gets the best of the bargain who trades Christ for anything. Whoever sells the Savior for any price is a fool. Whoever rejects the Savior for whatever enticement is the loser. Whoever accepts the false promises of sinful pleasure will live and die to mourn his folly.

Sin pays in counterfeit coin. Sin ends in disillusionment and death. To sell Jesus Christ, the Savior, is more foolish than a drowning man refusing to take the lifeboat; more foolhardy than the man in a burning building pushing away the ladder from the wall; more senseless than the man dying for lack of blood refusing a transfusion. What a fool Judas was! No wonder Jesus called him "the son of perdition" (John 17:12).

How lovingly Jesus bore with Judas during those three years! The Lord hath no pleasure in the death of the wicked. But the hard heart of Judas would not be broken, the stubborn will of Judas would not bend in submission to the Son of God. "Therefore the ungodly [in this case, Judas] shall not stand in the judgment, nor sinners in the congregation of the righteous." Judas is an ignominious illustration of ungodly men.

If you want to escape the condemnation of Judas, then you must do what Judas refused to do— you must trust Christ as your own personal Savior from sin. Yield to Him now.

> Jesus Christ, the King of kings and Lord of lords,
> Stands before you here. O heed His blessed Word.
> Will you trust Him Who to Heaven is the Door?
> Or will you by Him go to everlasting woe?

BLESSED SECURITY

I. The Omnipotence of Security

   A. His creation glorifies His power.
   B. His character guarantees His power.
   C. His conduct graces His power.

II. The Omniscience of Security

   A. He knows the identity of the way.
   B. He knows the individuals on the way.
   C. He knows the involvements along the way.

III. The Objects of Security

   A. An exclusive group
   B. An eternal group

CHAPTER SIX

Blessed Security

"For the LORD knoweth the way of the righteous; but the way of the ungodly shall perish" (Ps. 1:6).

SOCIAL SECURITY, economic security, collective security, national security. Security is a much-used word in the day and age in which we live. In this chapter we want to examine some of the passages of Scripture which have to do with *eternal security,* for this is the best security of all. Since we covered the character and plight of the ungodly in the last chapter, we will deal exclusively in this chapter with the first part of verse six, "The LORD knoweth the way of the righteous." In these eight words the psalmist gives us "Blessed Assurance" of eternal security.

I. The Omnipotence of Security

Solomon wrote: "The name of the LORD is a strong tower: the righteous runneth into it, and is safe" (Prov. 18:10). In another psalm, David praised the Lord with these words:

> The LORD is my rock, and my fortress, and my deliverer; my God, my strength, in whom I will trust; my buckler, and the horn of my salvation, and my high tower.

> I will call upon the LORD, who is worthy to be praised: so shall I be saved from mine enemies (Ps. 18:2, 3).

Where is the omnipotence, the almighty strength, for our security? IN THE LORD; not in armies, not in super bombs, not in man-made governments, not in money. We can say with Martin Luther:

A mighty fortress is our God, A bulwark never failing;
Our helper He amid the flood Of mortal ills prevailing.
For still our ancient foe Doth seek to work us woe—
His craft and pow'r are great, And, armed with cruel hate,
On earth is not his equal.

Did we in our own strength confide Our striving would be losing,
Were not the right Man on our side, The Man of God's own choosing.
Dost ask who that may be? Christ Jesus, it is He—
Lord Sabaoth His name, From age to age the same—
And He must win the battle.

And though this world, with devils filled, Should threaten to undo us,
We will not fear, for God hath willed His truth to triumph through us.
The prince of darkness grim— We tremble not for him;
His rage we can endure For lo! his doom is sure—
One little word shall fell him.

That word above all earthly pow'rs— No thanks to them— abideth;
The Spirit and the gifts are ours Through Him who with us sideth.
Let goods and kindred go, This mortal life also;
The body they may kill: God's truth abideth still—
His kingdom is forever.

We agree with Solomon the wise man, with David the king, with Luther the reformer— our security is in the Lord. The Lord is omnipotent, and this omnipotence, this power is promised to us through the Lord Jesus Christ. We already have adequate proof that the Lord's power is sufficient and available. The Word of God gives us three tremendous evidences of the availability of this power:

A. His creation glorifies His power.
B. His character guarantees His power.
C. His conduct graces His power.

First, His *creation glorifies His power*. David exclaims:

> The heavens declare the glory of God; and the firmament sheweth his handywork.
> Day unto day uttereth speech, and night unto night sheweth knowledge.
> There is no speech nor language, where their voice is not heard (Ps. 19:1-3).

The mighty power of God has been adequately demonstrated in the marvelous creation around us. God's creative ability is seen through the telescope; His infinite capacity for intricate detail is seen through the microscope; His careful workmanship is heard through the stethoscope.

The creation glorifies the power of God in many ways, but let us consider just three of the more apparent ways. Consider the *stuff* out of which He created all things. Hebrews 11:3 says: "Through faith we understand that the worlds were framed by the word of God, so that things which are seen were not made of things which do appear." What was God's source material? His Word!

The Hebrew word which is used in Genesis 1:1 for *create* means to "create out of nothing." God simply *spoke* this entire universe into existence. Fantastic? Not if God is omnipotent, and He is. Genesis 1 tells us, "God said, Let there be light: and there was light." Nine times in this first chapter of Genesis the words "God said" appear.

The Lord Jesus Christ demonstrated the power of the Word of God when He performed His miracles. He calmed the stormy sea by speaking to it. He raised Lazarus from the dead by simply speaking with the voice of omnipotence. He freed men from the enslavement of demons by ordering these demons with His authoritative voice of power. And the Christian may be confident of the power of God as displayed for us in the creation of a universe whose boundaries the telescopes of men have not as yet reached.

Compare the *stuff* with which God worked with that spiritual vacuum which you may possess in your life. Perhaps you are downcast because of your sin, because of the mess you have made of life, because of what you consider to be a lack of talent. But let us never forget that our God is able to take *nothing* and make *something* out of it. He is able to take Moses's rod and make it more powerful than the scepter of a Pharaoh. He is able to take David's slingshot and put to flight all of the armored might of the Philistines. He is able to take the little boy's five small loaves of bread and two fish and feed thousands of hungry people. Give God what you have and watch His masterful Hand make a thing of beauty and usefulness out of your nothingness. God delights to do this. Paul says that God takes the "base things of the world, and things which are despised . . . yea, and things which are not, to bring to nought things that are." Why? "That no flesh should glory in his presence" (1 Cor. 1:28, 29).

Next, consider the *speed* with which God created this majestic universe. Moses wrote:

> And God saw every thing that he had made, and, behold, it was very good. And the evening and the morning were the sixth day.
> Thus the heavens and the earth were finished, and all the host of them.
> For in six days the LORD made heaven and earth, the sea, and all that in them is, and rested the seventh day: wherefore the LORD blessed the sabbath day, and hallowed it (Gen. 1:31; 2:1; Exod. 20:11).

How long did it take God to bring this vast universe into being? SIX DAYS! What speed! What efficiency! What omnipotent power is shown in this length of time. I believe the days spoken of in Genesis 1 are literal 24-hour days. Nothing in the language or context indicates differently. God did all of this magnificent work in just six days. Don't ask me how. If I could tell you how, I would possess God's knowledge. But I believe He did!

When you possess any degree of knowledge at all of the vastness of this universe, of the manifold combinations of elements which have resulted in the millions of different substances which go into the makeup of this world, you must stand in awe that God could do all of this in six days. When you consider the length of time it took man to send a man to the moon, you can understand how the intelligence and power of God dwarf that of men. Think of the years of research and study and experimentation which preceded the moon landing. Add to these years for the building of machinery and factories which could manufacture parts for the equipment used. Think of the varied materials which went into the making of that equipment. The different metals, the complicated instruments, the fuels. It took man many years of study, work and failures before he finally succeeded in getting a man to the moon.

Then compare the size of a space capsule to our moon and see again how great our God is. Our capsule of a few tons compared to the moon is insignificant. But God threw into space celestial bodies so colossal as to make the moon look in comparison like a ball of yarn. Our little man-made capsule revolved in orbit around the moon, but think of the fantastic orbits in which some of God's celestial bodies revolve. For instance, Saturn revolves about the sun at a mean distance of 886,000,000 miles. And God created this enormous network, this grand universe in just six days. He made it and put it into operation in only 144 hours.

We do not intend to belittle the scientific and technological achievements of our age, but we do mean to glorify the infinitely greater power of our God. Let us never forget that the Author of the Bible is also the Author of true science. All of the materials with which we work were placed here by Him, and to Him we owe even the intelligence and ability which enables us to make such strides in rocketry and space travel. How thrilling it is to know that our "times are in His hands." How precious to know that the God Who can work with such mighty forces in such fantastic speed is guiding our lives day by day in every circumstance. Jesus said: "Are not two sparrows sold for a farthing? and one of them shall not fall on the ground without your Father. But the very hairs of your head are all numbered" (Matt. 10:29, 30).

Child of God, do you think that your life is so detailed and so loaded with cares that you can exhaust God? Do you think that God will become tired because you so often cry unto Him for help and counsel? Be sure that the God Who created and maintains this universe is able to keep you secure through the difficulties and dilemmas which encompass you.

Let us also consider the *soundness* of His creation. If precision work were ever done, it was done by God and continues to be done by God in His maintenance of the universe which He has created. God impressed Job with the soundness and with the greatness of His creation by asking Job some awesome questions:

> Canst thou bind the sweet influences of Pleiades, or loose the bands of Orion?
> Canst thou bring forth Mazzaroth in his season? or canst thou guide Arcturus with his sons?.
> Knowest thou the ordinances of heaven? canst thou set the dominion thereof in the earth?
> Canst thou lift up thy voice to the clouds, that abundance of water may cover thee? (Job 38:31-34).

On and on God goes with these searching questions to show Job the magnitude of the wisdom and knowledge of the Almighty.

Think of the soundness of this universe! Think of the thousands and thousands of years of time. Think of the wisdom of God in creating the sun at just the right distance, at just the right temperature, at just the right angle in order to bless the earth and not curse it. Think of the human body and the workmanship and wisdom which is incorporated into that body.

We take so much for granted! Just one part of the body

is enough to prove God's wisdom and soundness of judgment. The eye or the hand or the heart — every part of the body is wondrously made. And yet we use our bodies every day with hardly a thought as to the fact that we are living testimonials to the creative wisdom of an omnipotent God. You have probably used a telephone today. A telephone is quite an invention, is it not? Have you ever thought about what is involved in that telephone receiver you hold to your ear? Essentially, there are five parts: the receiver, the transmitter, the carbon granules, the magnet and the diaphragm. Did you know that? Yet you use that phone every day. But, wait; something is more amazing than the invention of the telephone, and that is the *ear* to which you place that telephone. Those two ears on your head are two good examples of the power and wisdom of God.

What would God have you *hear* with those ears? "Faith cometh by HEARING, and HEARING by the word of God" (Rom. 10:17). God says in Hebrews 3:7 and 8: "To day if ye will HEAR his voice, Harden not your hearts. . . ." There is a connection between the ear and the heart. God wants you to hear the message of the gospel, and He wants you to heed it. The God Whose mighty power created your ears and your heart assures you that He has the power to forgive your sins, to make you a new creation, to make your life worth living, to give you everlasting life, to give you real and rich security.

Second, God's *character guarantees His power* to the believer. A devoted father came into the room where his tiny boy was dying of an incurable disease. The child, sensing that he was not going to get well, asked his father, "Daddy, am I going to die?" "Why, son? Are you afraid to die?" The child looked up into the face of his father and replied, "Not if God is like you, Daddy!"

What gave this little child such confidence in his daddy and in God? This child knew the Christian character of his dad. He knew the truth of God just enough to know that because a person accepted Jesus as Savior, he possessed God as his Father. The little lad had also seen in his father such Christian grace that he felt secure in the care of the Heavenly Father just as he felt secure in the care of his earthly father.

The Scriptures tell us much about the attributes and character of our God and Savior. Because the character of God is truth and holiness, we can count on Him to keep His Word concerning our eternal safety. He promises eternal life to those who receive His Son, and the man is truly blessed who has this assurance. God's character is a subject in itself; so we will just mention in passing some of His attributes which make His promises of eternal salvation worthy of complete acceptation. God is eternal, infinite, immutable, all-wise, all-righteous, holy, faithful and gracious. The apostle Paul best expresses the confidence of the Blessed Man in the keeping power of God in Romans 8:35-39:

> Who shall separate us from the love of Christ? shall tribulation, or distress, or persecution, or famine, or nakedness, or peril, or sword?
>
> As it is written, For thy sake we are killed all the day long; we are accounted as sheep for the slaughter.
>
> Nay, in all these things we are more than conquerors through him that loved us.
>
> For I am persuaded, that neither death, nor life, nor angels, nor principalities, nor powers, nor things present, nor things to come,
>
> Nor height, nor depth, nor any other creature, shall be able to separate us from the love of God, which is in Christ Jesus our Lord.

This is the enduring and enjoyable assurance of every believer.

Third, history and the Word of God reveal that God's *conduct graces His power.* Never has God abused His omnipotence. Never has God acted contrary to His nature. Never has God done anything to cause reproach upon Himself. God may allow strange things to happen to the believer on the road of life, but God always has a purpose in those strange things. Paul assures us "that all things work together for good to them that love God, to them who are the called according to his purpose" (Rom. 8:28). All things are not necessarily good in themselves, but "all things *work together* for good" to God's people. Some of the ingredients which go into a cake are not very tasty when alone. Baking powder is not very palatable when by itself. A full tablespoon of vanilla extract would not make a delightful experience in taste. A raw egg or two may not be at all appetizing, but mix these individual ingredients together with a few more in the right proportions and bake it at the proper temperature and you have something that is good.

So God utilizes His omnipotence to bring all the varied experiences of our lives into something that can in every way be called good. He knows when sickness is needed; He knows when financial troubles should come; He knows how much prosperity we can safely take; so He mixes these things together and sees that we have the necessary heat of His sunshine or the fires of difficulties, and it all works out for good. This is what the psalmist had in mind when he wrote: "Surely the wrath of man shall praise thee: the remainder of wrath shalt thou restrain" (Ps. 76:10). William Cowper penned it beautifully:

God moves in a mysterious way,
His wonders to perform;
He plants His footsteps in the sea,
And rides upon the storm.

Ye fearful saints, fresh courage take;
The clouds ye so much dread
Are big with mercy, and shall break
In blessings on your head.

Judge not the Lord by feeble sense,
But trust Him for His grace;
Behind a frowning providence,
He hides a smiling face.

The Lord Jesus Christ taught His disciples that every experience of life has a meaning and a reason. One day the disciples followed the Lord out of the Temple, and they came by a blind man.

> And his disciples asked him, saying, Master, who did sin, this man, or his parents, that he was born blind?
> Jesus answered, Neither hath this man sinned, nor his parents: but that the works of God should be made manifest in him (John 9:2, 3).

There was a prime purpose in this blindness! And there is a purpose in your handicap — "that the works of God should be made manifest." There is such security in knowing that God never makes a mistake. If seeming tragedy strikes, there must be something better, something more precious that God wants to give us or do through us.

On another occasion, the Lord was informed that his friend Lazarus was gravely ill in Bethany. But instead of hurrying to his side, Jesus remained where He was until Lazarus had died. The reason for His delay is given in John 11:4: "When Jesus heard that, he said, This sickness is not unto death, but for the glory of God, that the Son of God might be glorified thereby." The disciples and the two sisters of Lazarus probably expected Jesus to glorify God by miraculously healing Lazarus. But Jesus had something even greater in mind. He would glorify God by raising Lazarus from the dead. Delay was not defeat. Delay meant greater victory. Jesus knew the purpose of God, and He magnified His God by perfect patience even when that waiting period was to bring sorrow to the hearts of some of His most dearly loved friends.

Paul testified to God's wisdom in working out the sometimes unexplainable events of life in the epistle to the Philippians.

> But I would ye should understand, brethren, that the things which happened unto me have fallen out rather unto the furtherance of the gospel.

According to my earnest expectation and my hope, that in nothing I shall be ashamed, but that with all boldness, as always, so now also Christ shall be magnified in my body, whether it be by life, or by death (Phil. 1:12, 20).

If Paul could have this confidence, certainly we need not despair. Paul lists some of the "all things" which "work together for good." "Of the Jews five times received I forty stripes save one. Thrice was I beaten with rods, once was I stoned, thrice I suffered shipwreck, a night and a day I have been in the deep" (2 Cor. 11:24, 25).

Thus it is that the Blessed Man can rest in the Lord Whose omnipotence insures him of blessed security.

II. The Omniscience of Security

"He's the biggest liar in Washington," Lincoln said about a well-known lawyer. "He reminds me of an old fisherman who got a reputation for stretching the truth. He got a pair of scales and insisted on weighing before witnesses each fish he caught. One day a doctor borrowed the scales to weigh a new baby. The baby weighted forty-seven pounds." This little story illustrates how men can be deceived. But God knows — implicitly, explicitly, always and ever! The God of Heaven and earth will never be fooled by any man. It is tragic foolishness for men to try so hard to pull the wool over the eyes of an all-seeing and all-knowing God.

Counterfeiting is a wicked and costly business. The vending machine industry takes in literally billions of dollars a year. If people could get away with using slugs, great sums of money could be lost every year. Because of this, vending machines have expensive and usually effective devices for detecting counterfeit coins. Every time a coin is put in the slot, the coin is automatically measured for thickness, diameter and metallic content; it is bounced to measure weight. If it does not meet the test, it is returned.

Counterfeiting is also going on in the realm of the spiritual. Satan is a deceiver, and there is no security in any of his subtle lies. The Devil may deceive individuals and he does. The Devil may deceive leaders and he does. The Devil may deceive nations and he does. But the Devil fails to deceive God. And those who follow the fabrications of the Devil likewise fail to deceive God. Paul says that Satan transforms himself into "an angel of light" (2 Cor. 11:14), but "be not deceived; God is not mocked" (Gal. 6:7). God knoweth the way of the righteous. He also knows what ways are not righteous, and He knows what people are not righteous. We can rest in His sure knowledge for three particular reasons as suggested by the psalmist.

First, *He knows the identity of the way.* Ralph Olson, a clerk at the state highway department's tourist information lodge in Menominee, Michigan, had a humorous experience. Mr. Olson said a woman stopped in and asked directions to a gas station. "What kind of gas do you want?" Olson asked. "Oh, I don't want any gas; I just want some tourist information," the woman replied.

This woman was like a great many people today with reference to the way to Heaven. Jesus said, "I am the way, the truth, and the life: no man cometh unto the Father, but by me" (John 14:6). The Way to God is a Person. They who are in Christ are in the Way of life everlasting. Jesus also said, "Strait is the gate, and narrow is the way, which leadeth unto life, and few there be that find it" (Matt. 7:14). This woman was asking the tourist information clerk to lead her to someone who could give her tourist information when all the time the man with all of the information was right in front of her! How many people today just cannot seem to accept the fact that Christ is ALL they need! They want to hear about Jesus, but they want to put their faith in their church. They want to be told about the Christ, but they want to trust their self-righteousness. They want to have someone preach to them about Christ the Burden-bearer, but they want to keep carrying their own load of worry. They claim to be "searching for the truth," yet they refuse to accept the very personified Truth Who is Jesus Christ.

The Bible tells us that Jesus is the only way to God; so

the individual who has trusted the Lord Jesus Christ as his Savior and Shepherd can be sure that God knows it and that God will accept him. The Blessed Man is safe and secure when he is in Christ the Way.

Second, *God knows the individuals on the way.* There are approximately four billion individuals in the world today. The infinite knowledge of our Savior takes in every minute detail of the lives of each of these four billion individuals. Such a capacity for knowledge is beyond human comprehension, yet the Word of God tells us that even the hairs of our heads are numbered. That is a blessed thought in relationship to each believer. In John 10:27-30 we read these words from the Lord Jesus Christ:

> My sheep hear my voice, and I know them, and they follow me:
> And I give unto them eternal life; and they shall never perish, neither shall any man pluck them out of my hand.
> My Father, which gave them me, is greater than all; and no man is able to pluck them out of my Father's hand.
> I and my Father are one.

In these verses we have some of the most precious promises of eternal security to be found in Scripture. The Lord Jesus Christ tells us that we have eternal life as a gift. He promises us that we shall *never* perish. He tells us that no other individual and no other power is able to change our eternal relationship to Him. He tells us that His Father is also pledged to keep us for eternal ages. What more security could a man want?

In this passage of Scripture the Lord Jesus calls us His sheep. As the Shepherd of the sheep, our Lord knows each of us individually. The apostle Paul enlarges upon this truth in 2 Timothy 2:19 where he writes: "Nevertheless the foundation of God standeth sure, having this seal, The Lord knoweth them that are his. And, Let every one that nameth the name of Christ depart from iniquity." Note particularly the phrase "the Lord knoweth them that are his." No believer is outside of the personal attentiveness of our Savior. This means that every believer can live with the absolute assurance that the Good Shepherd is interested in his every personal problem and need. It is this truth that makes prayer such a tremendous reality to the believer. Ten million believers may call upon God in prayer at the same time you are praying, but it is infinitely wonderful to know that God is able to give personal attention to you as an individual believer.

It is also true that since the Lord Jesus Christ knows the righteous individually, He is able to direct the circumstances of each life so that every believer can be used to his greatest potential to the glory of his Savior. The twelve apostles were men of different temperaments, diverse abilities and varied backgrounds. Yet the Lord knew each of these men could do a special job. So He called these men with a knowledge that their ministries would result in the success of the preaching of the gospel of Jesus Christ to the then-known world. This reminds us of what Paul wrote in 1 Corinthians 12:4-7:

> Now there are diversities of gifts, but the same Spirit.
> And there are differences of administrations, but the same Lord.
> And there are diversities of operations, but it is the same God which worketh all in all.
> But the manifestation of the Spirit is given to every man to profit withal.

Therefore, it is up to each individual believer to yield himself to God. God will take the yielded life and use it where He sees best and how He sees best.

In John 2:24 and 25 we read: "But Jesus did not commit himself unto them, because he knew all men, And needed not that any should testify of man: for he knew what was in man." You cannot fool the Good Shepherd. He knows whether or not you are one of His sheep. He is not fooled by your outward appearance nor by your outward profession. He knows your heart. He knows what is in you. He knows your thoughts, and it is tremendously important that you be open and honest before God. If you are not a Christian, now is the time to sincerely and honestly invite the Lord Jesus Christ into your heart as your personal Savior. Allow Him to cleanse your heart and life from the sin that has festered there for so long. Do not be as the Pharisees whom the Lord Jesus Christ described as "whited sepulchres." They look nice on the outside but within are full of dead men's bones.

If you are a Christian, are you living in obedience to your Savior? Is He pleased with what He sees in your life? Is He pleased with what He reads in your mind? Is He pleased with what He hears from your lips? Is He pleased with the places you frequent? For you see, my friend, the Lord Jesus Christ does know all of these things about you. He knows the way of the righteous, and He knows the persons who are in that way. It is because of the omniscience of our great God that the judgment will be a time of infinitely righteous justice.

Third, *God knows the involvements along the way.* The individual believer does not have to fear the changing tides and circumstances of this world's political setup. Nations rise and fall; leaders come to power and go down in disgrace; personalities roar across the skies of popularity like meteors; and it seems that the world's stability is about to collapse in universal confusion. But amid all of this the believer can be serenely secure with the knowledge that Jesus Christ knows all about these circumstances. The apostle Paul wrote to Timothy from prison and summarized his situation from his jail cell in these words:

> At my first answer no man stood with me, but all men forsook me: I pray God that it may not be laid to their charge.
> Notwithstanding the Lord stood with me, and strengthened me; that by me the preaching might be fully known, and that all the Gentiles might hear: and I was delivered out of the mouth of the lion.

And the Lord shall deliver me from every evil work, and will preserve me unto his heavenly kingdom: to whom be glory for ever and ever. Amen (2 Tim. 4:16-18).

Note three things in these verses. First of all, along the way the believer will come into contact with many *persons*. Some of these people will endeavor to do harm to the believer. Some of these persons will do their best to help the believer, and still others of these persons will be absolutely indifferent to the needs or desires of the believer. In all of these instances the Lord will see to it that each contact will glorify the Lord Jesus Christ and be of help to the believer in doing the will of God. I do not believe that any Christian ever comes in contact with another individual without there being some purpose in that contact. In these verses Paul said that at first "no man stood with me." This was no doubt a sad day in the life of the apostle Paul, and yet what a joy it must have been to him to know that his God could overrule the frailties and failures of his human enemies.

Second, along the way the believer will find that his circumstances aid him in *preaching*. The apostle wrote, "Notwithstanding the Lord stood with me, and strengthened me; that by me the preaching might be fully known. . . ." The believer's life ought to be a life of preaching the gospel. Every event, every circumstance, every sorrow, every occasion of joy, every prosperity and every adversity ought to be an opportunity to testify somehow to the grace of God. The apostle Paul was a master at this. He wrote in Philippians 4:11: "Not that I speak in respect of want: for I have learned, in whatsoever state I am, therewith to be content." When the apostle Paul was hauled before magistrates and kings, he took it as an occasion to preach the gospel. When the apostle Paul was chained in a dungeon, he took it as an occasion to have a midnight praise service at which time he led the jailor to Christ. When the apostle Paul found himself shipwrecked on an island, he took the occasion to have a special series of evangelistic meetings. When he found himself in Rome as a prisoner, he took the occasion to convert his prison quarters into a mission station. Always and in every place the apostle Paul preached.

We can be sure that our Savior will see to it that all of the involvements of our lives give opportunity to be a witness. That is why every believer ought always to be prepared. That is why we should always be alert to say a word for our Savior. That is why we need to live in close communion with our Lord, so that the Holy Spirit can lead us each moment to be a blessing to those with whom we are involved in life's daily round of activities.

Third, along the way the believer can be certain of *preservation*. In 2 Timothy 4:18 the apostle Paul wrote with complete assurance: "And the Lord shall deliver me from every evil work, and will preserve me unto his heavenly kingdom." This is the assurance of every believer. As long as he is in the will of God and as long as God has a job for him to do, no fire can burn him, no water can drown him, no slander can still him, no army can stay him and no power in Heaven or on earth or in Hell can conquer him. This is the blessed security of the believer in the omniscience of his Savior.

III. The Objects of Security

We complete this exposition of our blessed security by calling attention to the fact that the omnipotence and omniscience of our blessed Lord are pledged to a very exclusive group of people. The Scriptures reveal this group as "the righteous." It is important that we understand the term *righteous*. We are not referring to man's righteousness. Neither are we referring to the righteousness which comes by striving to keep the Law. Nor are we referring to a moral righteousness in which man may pride himself. We are referring to a righteousness which is bestowed upon or imputed to an individual when he by faith accepts the Lord Jesus Christ as his Savior. In 2 Corinthians 5:21 we read: "For he [God] hath made him [Christ] to be sin for us, who

[Christ] knew no sin; that we might be made the righteousness of God in him [Christ]." In other words, the Lord Jesus Christ takes our sin, and we take His righteousness. When the Scriptures refer to the righteous, they are only referring to those who possess the righteousness of God. Christ in God is pledged to preserve those who are in Christ through all eternity.

All that we have said in this chapter concerning the omnipotence of God, the omniscience of God, the grace of God and the entire character of God, bears on this one point — that the righteous are secure in this God. All that God has, all that God is, all that God will ever do and all that God promises, guarantees everlasting security for the believer. The righteousness of God in Christ is a possession of every believer.

First John 1:9 tells us that God is "faithful" and "just." Now the question is, To whom is He faithful and to whom is He just? God is faithful to the Lord Jesus Christ, and God is just on the behalf of the Lord Jesus Christ in forgiving us our sins and in cleansing us from all unrighteousness when we accept the Savior. For it is the righteousness of Christ imputed to us which brings all of the forces of God to bear in our behalf and in behalf of our eternal security. That is why Jude wrote:

> Now unto him that is able to keep you from falling, and to present you faultless before the presence of his glory with exceeding joy,
> To the only wise God our Saviour, be glory and majesty, dominion and power, both now and ever. Amen (Jude 24, 25).

Notice in this passage of Scripture that the believer is the object of the verbs. Jude writes that He will keep *you;* He will present *you*. In other words, the believer is the object of God's keeping power. We as believers are the recipients of God's grace, of God's guarantee, and of God's gifts. Such blessed security causes us to sing:

More secure is no one ever
Than the loved ones of the Savior—
Not yon star on high abiding
Nor the bird in homenest hiding.

God His own doth tend and nourish,
In His holy courts they flourish;
Like a father kind He spares them,
In His loving arms He bears them.

Neither life nor death can ever
From the Lord His children sever,
For His love and deep compassion
Comforts them in tribulation.

Little flock, to joy then yield thee!
Jacob's God will ever shield thee;
Rest secure with this Defender—
At His will all foes surrender.

What He takes or what He gives us
Shows the Father's love so precious;
We may trust His purpose wholly—
'Tis His children's welfare solely.

Thus we see that the God-blessed man is a man of blessed separation; a man of blessed study; a man of blessed stability; a man who has escaped the tragedies of baneful stubble and baneful shame; and a man who lives in the blessed security of the great Savior with Whom he walks. As you walk in such scriptural manner, may God bless you!